How to Use
The Little Penguin Handbook

Examine the **Brief Contents** on the inside front cover. Find a general subject and then flip to the corresponding part. Each chapter is identified by a small image; look for that image at the top of the page within each part.

Check the flap inside the back cover. You'll find a list of **Common Errors** that many writers make. Scan the list for the problems you want to solve, and then use the page number to find the relevant Common Errors box.

Open the back cover. You'll see a **detailed table of contents** that includes the chapter topics and the main divisions of each chapter. Use the page numbers to find your topic.

Turn to the **index** beginning on page 266. It lists the page numbers of every topic in the handbook.

Use the **Glossary of Grammatical Terms and Usage** (page 255) to find the meaning of a basic grammatical term or an explanation of how to use confusing words.

Find information about MLA, APA, CMS, or CSE **documentation styles** for research writing by turning to the first page of each chapter in Part 3, where you will find a complete index of sample citations for each documentation style.

Writing Across the Curriculum

You can quickly locate information related to Writing Across the Curriculum by using the list below. In addition to resources for specific disciplines, this page highlights topics that cross disciplines or extend to public and professional contexts.

THE
Little Penguin Handbook

LESTER FAIGLEY

UNIVERSITY OF TEXAS AT AUSTIN

New York   San Francisco   Boston
London   Toronto   Sydney   Tokyo   Singapore   Madrid
Mexico City   Munich   Paris   Cape Town   Hong Kong   Montreal

Senior Acquisitions Editor: Lynn M. Huddon
Development Editor: Michael S. Greer
Executive Marketing Manager: Megan Galvin-Fak
Production Manager: Bob Ginsberg
Project Coordination, Text Design, and Electronic Page Makeup: Pre-Press Company, Inc.
Cover Design Manager: Nancy Danahy
Cover Photos: © Getty Images, Inc.
Senior Manufacturing Buyer: Dennis J. Para
Printer and Binder: Webcrafters, Inc.
Cover Printer: Phoenix Color Corporation

Library of Congress Cataloging-in-Publication Data

Faigley, Lester, 1947–
    The little Penguin handbook / Lester Faigley.-- 1st ed.
        p. cm.
    Abbreviated version of The Penguin handbook.
    Includes bibliographical references and index.
    ISBN 0-321-24401-X (alk. paper)
  1. English language—Rhetoric—Handbooks, manuals, etc. 2. English language—Grammar—
Handbooks, manuals, etc. 3. Report writing—Handbooks, manuals, etc. I. Faigley, Lester, 1947–
Penguin handbook. II. Title.
PE1408.F245 2006
808'.042—dc22   2005030270

Visit us at www.ablongman.com

ISBN 0-321-24401-X

4 5 6 7 8 9 10 — WC — 09 08 07

PART ONE

Composing

CHAPTER 1
The Rhetorical Situation

1a THE RHETORICAL TRIANGLE

Whether you are writing a research paper for a political science course, designing a Web site for a small business, or preparing slides for a sales presentation, you are participating in a complex process. That process—communication—involves the interaction of three essential elements: the writer or speaker, the audience, and the subject. These three elements are often represented by a triangle.

Speaker, subject, and audience are each necessary for an act of communication to occur. These three elements interact with each other. Speakers make adjustments to their presentations of a subject depending on the audience (think of how you talk to small children). Just as speakers adjust to audiences, audiences continually adjust to speakers (think of how your attitude toward speakers changes when they are able to laugh at themselves).

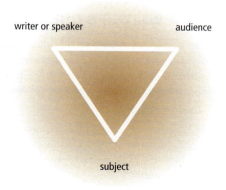

writer or speaker   audience

subject

FIGURE 1.1 The rhetorical triangle

1b A WRITER'S AUDIENCE

In college writing, you often write for readers you know directly, including your classmates and your teachers. In the workplace, you may not always know who is going to read your reports or memos. Ask yourself who will read your writing and think about what kind of information you need to provide to engage them.

Understand your audience

1. Who is most likely to read what you write?
2. How much does your audience know about your subject? Are there any key terms or concepts that you will need to explain?
3. How interested is your audience likely to be? If they lack interest in your subject, how can you get them engaged?
4. What is their attitude likely to be toward your subject? If they hold attitudes different from yours, how can you get them to consider your views?
5. What would motivate your audience to want to read what you write?

1c A WRITER'S CREDIBILITY

Some writers begin with credibility because of who they are. Most writers, however, have to convince their readers to keep reading by demonstrating knowledge of their subject and concern with their readers' needs.

Build your credibility

1. How can you convince your audience that you are knowledgeable about your subject? Do you need to do research?
2. How can you convince your audience that you have their interests in mind?
3. What strategies can you use that will enhance your credibility? Should you cite experts on your subject? Can you acknowledge opposing positions, indicating that you've taken a balanced view on your subject?
4. Does the appearance, accuracy, and clarity of your writing give you credibility?

1d A WRITER'S PURPOSE

Most writing you will do falls into one of three categories: **reflective**, **informative**, or **persuasive**. Your purpose will shape the style, organization, and design of your writing.

Purposes for writing

Reflective

- Personal letters and personal email maintain relationships and family ties.
- Personal essays offer the writer's feelings about people, places, and experiences.
- Travel narratives describe the experiences of individuals in unfamiliar places.

Informative

- Business letters inform clients, customers, and employees of products and policies.
- Newspaper and magazine articles report events, sports, entertainment, and other topics.
- Brochures inform people about organizations and services.
- Reports of experiments, case studies, surveys, and observations present new knowledge.

Persuasive

- Letters of application and résumés try to convince an employer or institution to interview the applicant.
- Advertisements seek to persuade consumers to purchase products and services.
- Position arguments make a claim about a controversial issue.
- Proposal arguments recommend a course of action in response to a recognizable problem.

 CHAPTER 2

Communicating with Words, Images, and Graphics

Knowing when to use images and graphics and when to use words requires you to think about them as media—as different means of conveying information and ideas. Many ideas and concepts can be explained more effectively with a combination of words, graphics, and images.

2a ORGANIZATION IN VERBAL TEXTS

Organization is the path the writer creates for readers to follow. Even in a reference book like this one, in which readers consult particular chapters and sections according to their needs, there is still a path from beginning to end. Sentences, paragraphs, sections, and chapters are the writer's materials in constructing the pathway. The writer creates a pathway in words to take readers to particular subjects, much as a trail leads to different places. If the trail is well marked and the places identified, the reader can follow without getting lost and can revisit particular places.

Mapping of ideas

Some kinds of writing demand particular kinds of organization. A short memo in an office typically begins with an announcement of the subject. But in other kinds of writing, the organization is not so predictable. How you begin and how you take the reader along a pathway depends on what you are trying to achieve. Thinking about your purpose often helps you to map out the organization.

Titles, headings, and paragraphs

Titles and headings combine verbal and visual indicators of levels of importance and major divisions in subject matter. Paragraphs give visual cues to the progression of ideas in verbal texts. Other visual indicators such as **boldface** and *italics* provide emphasis at the level of words and phrases. Print, after all, is a visual as well as a verbal medium.

John Wesley Powell—early life

1834–born in Ohio, son of a Methodist minister
1846–moved to Wisconsin, educated himself in science
1857–traveled down Mississippi River in rowboat

John Wesley Powell—after Civil War

1867–1st expedition to Colorado
1868–spent winter among the Utes
1868–unsuccessful attempt for government support
     for expedition

John Wesley Powell—first descent of the Grand Canyon

1869, May 24–left from Green River, Wyoming
1869, June 9–lost boat at Disaster Falls
1869, August–descended Grand Canyon low on food
1869, August 28–3 men quit trip at the last major rapid

John Wesley Powell—later career

1871–2nd expedition down Colorado River,
     brought photographer
1878–published Arid Lands
1879–director of the Bureau of Ethnology
1881–director of U.S. Geological Survey

Notecards are a traditional method for mapping ideas.

2b ORGANIZATION IN VISUAL TEXTS

Organization is often called *composition* by photographers, artists, and designers. The materials for photographers and artists are objects placed in space.

Both of the pictures below are of the same subject. Which do you find more appealing—the image on the left or the one on the right?

Static versus dynamic

The image on the left is a typical snapshot. The person is placed at the exact center and the horizon is about at the midpoint. Putting the subject in the exact center is typical of people who take snapshots without thinking about how they are composed. The effect is static because the focus is on the object.

The image on the right moves the person away from the center and places him in relation to a large rock illuminated by the setting sun. Instead of focusing on the man, we now see him in relation to objects on the beach and the sea and sky behind.

If the picture is divided into thirds horizontally and vertically, we can see that the prominent rock and the man are placed at the intersections of these imaginary lines. This principle of organization is known as the "rule of thirds." While there is no beginning and ending in a photograph, principles of organization still apply.

2c POINT OF VIEW IN VERBAL TEXTS

At the most basic level, point of view means selecting among first person (*I, we*), second person (*you*), and third person (*he, she, it*) when you write about your subject. Using *I* emphasizes the writer or the teller of the story in fiction. Using *you* puts the relationship between writer and reader in the foreground. Using *he, she,* or *it* keeps the focus more on the subject and diminishes the prominence of the writer.

Point of view is also determined by how you locate yourself in relation to your subject. Whether you write in first or third person, you can write about a subject from close, firsthand experience or you can place yourself at a distance from your subject, giving the sense of being an impartial observer offering an overview.

You can write about the Grand Canyon as if you were looking out from the window of an airplane.

The Grand Canyon is 218 miles long, from 4 to 18 miles wide, and over a mile deep in some places. From the sky the contrast between the north and

south rims of the Grand Canyon is striking. The north rim is above 9,000 feet and covered by a thick forest; the south rim is about 1,200 feet lower than the north rim and has much less vegetation. The bottom of the canyon is the northernmost extension of the Sonoran Desert, where several different species of cacti, thistle, and other desert plants are found.

You can write about the Grand Canyon from the bottom.

On a late afternoon in August with the temperature well over 100°, we paddled our kayaks into Elves Chasm after getting pounded most of the day by some of the biggest rapids in the Grand Canyon—Granite, Hermit, Crystal, Serpentine, and Waltenberg—taking our casualties in turbulent swims when rolls failed. The cool trickle from the waterfall brought relief to the scorching canyon. The droplets glistened on the intense green moss and ferns like thousands of gems.

2d POINT OF VIEW IN VISUAL TEXTS

Where we choose to stand when we take a photograph makes all the difference in how the audience sees the subject. The photographer gives the audience a vantage point to take in the subject by allowing the audience to see what the photographer sees, creating an effect comparable to the use of *I* in writing. But photographers can also diminish the immediacy of a photograph by placing subjects at a distance or photographing them in stereotypical ways.

Three views of a bullpen

The bullpen is the part of a baseball park where relief pitchers warm up and wait their turn to pitch. What difference does point of view make in how we see the bullpen?

Photographers also create a *you* relationship with their subjects. Photographing people at close range creates a sense of interaction between subject and photographer.

CHAPTER 3

Critical Reading and Viewing

Most of the writing you will do in college and the workplace requires you to reflect in depth on what you read, a process called **critical reading.** This awareness does not stop with reading. College courses also ask you to engage in critical viewing, to think in depth about what you see—whether it be in the form of photographs, drawings, paintings, graphics, advertising, television, film, or the World Wide Web.

3a CRITICAL READING

When you read the work of several people in the same discipline, you quickly realize that they do not have the same point of view; they may not even agree on basic facts. And you also quickly realize that their work builds on the work of others; thus you have to have a sense of how they are interpreting the work of others before you can evaluate their claims. You can become a more effective critical reader if you have a set of strategies and use them while you read.

Previewing

No subject is ever completely new; likely many people have written and talked about the subject and many have views on the subject. First, think about why the writer chose the particular subject, why the piece of writing was published, and who were the intended readers. Begin by asking the following questions:

- Who wrote this material?
- Where did it first appear? In a book, newspaper, magazine, or online?
- What is the topic or issue?
- Where does the writer stand on the topic or issue?
- What else has been written about the topic or issue?
- Why was it written?

Summarizing

Make sure you understand exactly what is at issue. Circle any words or references that you don't know and look them up. You may get a sense of the

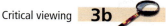

main points the first time through, or you may have to read the piece slowly a second time. Summarize by asking yourself these questions:

- What is the writer's main claim or question?
- If you do not find a specific claim, what is the main focus?
- What are the key ideas or concepts that the writer considers?
- What are the key terms? How does the writer define those terms?

Analyzing

On your second reading, start analyzing the structure, using the following questions:

- How is the piece of writing organized?
- What does the writer assume the readers know and believe?
- Where is the evidence? Can you think of contradictory evidence?
- Does the writer refer to expert opinion or research about this subject?
- Does the writer acknowledge opposing views? Does the writer deal fairly with opposing views?
- What kinds of sources are cited? Are they thoroughly documented?
- How does the writer represent herself or himself?

Responding

As you read, write down your thoughts. Something you read may remind you of something else. Jot that down. Ask yourself these questions:

- To what points made by the writer should I respond?
- What ideas might be developed or interpreted differently?
- What do I need to look up?
- What else should I read before writing?

3b CRITICAL VIEWING

Like critical reading, critical viewing requires you to reflect in depth on what you see. Use the following strategies while you analyze photographs, advertisements, and other visuals.

3b Critical Reading and Viewing

Previewing

Critical viewing requires thinking about the context first.

- Who created this image?
- Why was it created?
- Where and when did it first appear?
- What media are used?
- What has been written about the creator or the image?

Analyzing

The following analytical questions apply primarily to still images. Animations and motion pictures also provoke questions about their narrative structure.

- How is the image composed or framed?
- Where do my eyes go first? If there is an attention-grabbing element, how does it connect with the rest of the image?
- How is color used?
- How does the image appeal to the values of the audience?
- Was it intended to serve a purpose besides art or entertainment?

Responding

Make notes and write as and after you view the image, with these questions in mind:

- What was my first impression of the image?
- After thinking more—perhaps reading more—about it, how has that first impression changed or expanded?

We can analyze the photo on the opposite page by considering its context. The Southern Pacific billboard suggests that the picture was taken when travel by train was still popular. In fact, this photograph was taken in 1937 by Dorothea Lange (1895–1965), who gave it the title "Toward Los Angeles, California." We can also note significant details about the composition of the photo. The lines of the shoulder of the road, the highway, and the telephone poles slope toward a vanishing point on the horizon, giving a sense of great distance. The two figures in dark clothing walking away contrast to a rectangular billboard with a white background and white frame.

Another approach to critical viewing is to analyze the content. In 1937 the United States was in the midst of the Great Depression and a severe drought, which forced many small farmers in middle America to abandon their homes and go to California in search of work. By placing the figures and the billboard beside each other (a visual relationship called juxtaposition), Lange is able to make an ironic commentary on the lives of well-off and poor Americans during the Depression.

 C H A P T E R   4

Planning

Good architects begin by asking who will use a building and what they will use it for. Good writers ask similar questions: Who is likely to read what I write? What am I trying to accomplish? How do I anticipate that readers will be influenced by what I write? Will they know something they didn't know before? Will they consider taking some action based on what I have written?

4a LOOK CAREFULLY AT THE ASSIGNMENT

Often an assignment will contain key words such as *analyze, compare and contrast, define, describe, evaluate,* or *propose* that will assist you in identifying your purpose and goals.

- **Analyze:** Find connections among a set of facts, events, or readings, and make them meaningful.
- **Compare and contrast:** Examine how two or more things are alike and how they differ.
- **Define:** Make a claim about how something should be defined.
- **Describe:** Observe carefully and select details that create a dominant impression.
- **Evaluate:** Argue that something is good, bad, best, or worst, according to criteria that you set out.
- **Propose:** Identify a particular problem and explain why your solution is the best one.

4b FIND A TOPIC AND WRITE A WORKING THESIS

Having a specific focus is the key to writing a strong essay.

Use questions to focus a broad topic

Childhood obesity might be a current and interesting research topic, but it is too broad. Ask questions that will break a big topic into smaller topics.

- Why are children becoming obese?
- Why are children today more obese than children of past generations?
- How has the American food industry contributed to childhood obesity?
- What changes in American culture have contributed to childhood obesity?
- What are the adverse health effects of childhood obesity?
- What strategies are effective for preventing childhood obesity?

Consider other angles to expand a narrow topic

Sometimes a topic can become too narrow or limiting. Although candy consumption may be one contributing factor leading to obesity in children, this narrow focus overlooks other factors that together lead to childhood obesity. For instance:

- Why do some children eat large amounts of candy yet maintain a healthy weight?
- Children have always eaten candy. Why are children today more obese than children of past generations?
- Even when parents keep kids away from candy, some still gain weight. Why?

Considering counterarguments can help you expand your topic before you construct your working thesis.

Turn your topic into a thesis statement

Your thesis states your main idea. Much of the writing that you will do in college and in your career will have an explicit thesis, usually stated near the beginning. Your thesis should be closely tied to your purpose—to reflect on your own experience, to explain some aspect of your topic, or to argue for a position or course of action.

A REFLECTIVE THESIS
Watching my younger sister's struggles with her weight has taught me that childhood obesity has long-lasting psychological effects that can carry over into adulthood for many people.

AN INFORMATIVE THESIS
Childhood obesity has continued to increase over the past decade despite increasing awareness of its detrimental effects.

A PERSUASIVE THESIS
Parents must take a leading role in encouraging healthy eating and exercise habits in order to reverse the growing trend toward obesity in children.

CHAPTER 5

Drafting

Successful writers are aware of what they will need to do to complete a writing task, and they have strategies for when they get stuck or encounter the unexpected.

5a DETERMINE YOUR ORGANIZATION

Working outlines

A working outline is more like an initial sketch of how you will arrange the major sections. Jotting down main points and a few subpoints before you begin can be a great help while you are writing.

Formal outlines

A formal outline typically begins with the thesis statement, which anchors the entire outline. Each numbered or lettered item clearly supports the thesis, and the relationship among the items is clear from the outline hierarchy. Roman numerals indicate the highest level; next come capital letters, then numbers, and finally lowercase letters. The rule to remember when deciding whether you need to use the next level down is that each level must have at least two items: a "1." needs a "2."; an "a." needs a "b." Formal outlines can be helpful because they force you to look carefully at your organization.

Discipline-specific organization

In the social sciences, research reports typically follow a specific organization, with an abstract that gives a brief summary of the contents followed by four main sections and a list of references. This organization allows other researchers to identify information quickly.

1. The **introduction** (identifies the problem, reviews previous research, and states the hypothesis that was tested)
2. The **methods section** (describes how the experiment was conducted and how the participants were selected)

3. The **results section** (reports the findings of the study. This section often includes tables and figures that provide statistical results and tests of statistical significance)
4. The **discussion section** (interprets the findings and often refers to previous research)

Similarly, a lab report in the sciences or engineering will usually have the following organization with these distinct parts:

1. Abstract (gives a summary of the report)
2. Introduction (gives the purpose and background of the experiment)
3. Methods and Materials (refers to the lab manual used)
4. Procedure (describes what was actually done in the experiment)
5. Results (states results in both sentence and graphic form)
6. Discussion (includes an analysis of what can be explained from the results)
7. Conclusion (states what is known from the experiment)

5b COMPOSE A DRAFT

Essays typically contain an introduction, body, and conclusion. You do not have to draft these parts in that order, though. You may want to begin with your best example, which might be in the third paragraph according to your informal or working outline. The most important thing about drafting is that you feel comfortable and treat yourself kindly. If the inner critic shows up—that little voice in your mind that has nothing encouraging to say—banish it, refute it, write through it.

Overcoming writer's block

- If you have an outline, put it on the computer screen or place it beside you.
- Begin writing what you know best.
- Resist the urge to revise too soon.
- If you get stuck, try working on another section.
- If you are still stuck, talk to someone about what you are trying to write.

CHAPTER 6

Composing Paragraphs

You may have heard a paragraph defined as a unit of thought, but that definition is incomplete. A paragraph is also a device to help readers. Most readers today cringe at the sight of paragraphs that fill entire pages, and, as a result, paragraphs have become shorter over the past hundred years. Most important, readers expect that the sequence of paragraphs will set out a line of thought that they can follow.

6a FOCUS YOUR PARAGRAPHS

Readers expect sentences in a paragraph to be closely related to one another. Often writers will begin a paragraph with one idea, but other ideas will occur to them while they are writing. Paragraphs confuse readers when they go in different directions. When you revise your paragraphs, check for focus.

Topic sentences

You were probably taught to begin each paragraph with a topic sentence. Topic sentences alert readers to the focus of a paragraph and help writers stay on topic. Topic sentences should explain the focus of the paragraph and situate it in the larger argument. Topic sentences, however, do not have to begin paragraphs, and they need not be just one sentence. You will decide what placement and length will best suit your subject.

6b ORGANIZE YOUR PARAGRAPHS

Well-organized paragraphs in essays usually follow a pattern similar to that of a well-organized paper, but in miniature. Three strategies for effectively organizing sentences within a paragraph follow. Remember, the form of the paragraph should follow its function in the paper. Chances are you'll use a combination of these strategies within paragraphs in order to get your point across.

NARRATION OR PROCESS

Narrative paragraphs tell a story for a reason. Organized by time, narratives relate a series of events in the order they occur. This approach is useful when the temporal order of ideas or events is essential to their logic, such as in how-to writing.

The ascent goes easier than they expected. In two hours they reach the yak pastures where they will make the high camp. The view from the high camp is spectacular, with Dhaulagiri in clouds above them and the three sunlit summits of Nilgiri across the valley, with snow plumes blowing from their tops. Jim and Lester drop their packs at the campsite and continue walking to scout the route above the camp that they will follow in the darkness of early morning the next day. They find a steep path that parallels a fern-lined gorge, now rich in fall color. It is the lushest forest they have seen in Nepal. They congratulate each other on their decision to attempt to climb to the Dhaulagiri icefall, unaware that they will soon experience the mountain's furious weather, even on its lower slopes.

Verbs establish the sequence of events to orient the reader in time.

Narrative paragraphs often include description to orient the reader in space.

COMPARISON AND CONTRAST

Paragraphs of comparison assess one subject in terms of its relation to others, usually highlighting what they have in common. Contrasting paragraphs analyze differences between things.

You can organize a comparison or a contrast in two ways: by describing one thing and then describing another, or by moving back and forth between the two items point by point. Often the latter strategy highlights contrasts, as the following paragraph illustrates.

Establishes the terms of the comparison

Each phrase shows the medieval "heart" and the "thin" overlay of Western culture.

Nepal was closed to Europeans from 1843 to 1949 and missed the colonial influences of the British. Consequently, Kathmandu remains a medieval city at heart, with a thin overlay of the last two decades of trendy Western culture: Tibetan women dressed in traditional clothes weave rugs on antique looms while humming Sting tunes; a traffic jam on Kathmandu's only wide street is caused by bulls fighting in an intersection; restaurants play U2 and serve tough buffalo steak under the name *chateau briande;* coffee houses serve cappuccino across the street from women drying rice by lifting it into the air with hoes; nearly naked children wearing burlap sacks grab cake slices out of the hands of gawking tourists emerging from a Viennese pastry shop.

This comparison/ contrast also uses a cause-and-effect pattern to help organize it. The word *consequently* in the third line is the transition from the cause to the effect.

CAUSE AND EFFECT

Cause-and-effect paragraphs are structured in two basic ways. The paragraph can begin with a cause or causes, then state its effects, or it can begin with an effect, then state its causes. Insightful analysis often requires you to look beyond the obvious to the underlying causes.

The loss of the world's forests affects every country through global warming, decreased biodiversity, and soil erosion, but few suffer its impact more than Nepal. Deforestation in Nepal has led to economic stagnation and further depletion of forest resources. The immediate cause of deforestation is the need for more fuel and more farmland by an increasing population. The loss of trees in Nepal, however, has been accelerated by government policies. During the eighteenth and nineteenth centuries, Nepal taxed both land and labor. Farmers could avoid these high taxes for three years if they converted forests to farmland. Others could pay their taxes in firewood or charcoal. While these taxes were reduced in the twentieth century, the government required farmers to register their land, which encouraged clearing of trees to establish boundaries. Furthermore, the stagnant economy led to families' wanting more children to help in the fields at home and to send abroad to find jobs as another source of income.

Effects

Obvious cause

Underlying cause 1

Underlying cause 2

Underlying cause 3

6c WRITE EFFECTIVE BEGINNING AND ENDING PARAGRAPHS

Effective beginning paragraphs convince the reader to read on. They capture the reader's interest and set the tone for the piece.

Start beginning paragraphs with a bang

Try beginning with one of the following strategies to get your reader's attention.

A QUESTION
How valuable are snow leopards? The director of a zoo in Darjeeling, India, was fired when its snow leopard caught a cold and died.

IMAGES
Tons of animal pelts and bones sit in storage at Royal Chitwan National Park in Nepal. The mounds of poached animal parts confiscated by forest rangers reach almost to the ceiling. The air is stifling, the stench stomach-churning.

A PROBLEM
Ecologists worry that the construction of a natural gas pipeline in Russia's Ukok Plateau will destroy the habitat of endangered snow leopards, argali mountain sheep, and steppe eagles.

A CONCISELY STATED THESIS
If the governments of China and Russia don't soon act decisively, snow leopards will be extinct in a few years.

Conclude with strength

Ending paragraphs remind readers where they've been and invite them to carry your ideas forward. Use the ending paragraph to touch on your key points, but do not merely summarize. Leave your readers with something that will inspire them to continue to think about what you have written.

ISSUE A CALL TO ACTION
Although ecological problems in Russia seem distant, students like you and me can help protect the snow leopard by joining the World Wildlife Fund campaign.

MAKE RECOMMENDATIONS

Russia's creditors would be wise to sign on to the World Wildlife Fund's proposal to relieve some of the country's debt in order to protect snow leopard habitat. After all, if Russia is going to be economically viable, it needs to be ecologically healthy.

SPECULATE ABOUT THE FUTURE

Unless Nepali and Chinese officials devote more resources to snow leopard preservation, these beautiful animals will be gone in a few years.

CHAPTER 7

Revising, Editing, and Proofreading

The secret to writing well is rewriting. Even the best writers have to revise several times to get the result they want. You need effective strategies for revising if you're going to be successful. The biggest trap you can fall into is starting with the little stuff. *Don't sweat the small stuff at the beginning.*

7a EVALUATE YOUR DRAFT

Use the following questions to evaluate your draft. Note any places where you might make improvements.

- Does your paper or project meet the assignment?
- Does your writing have a clear focus?
- Are your main points adequately developed?
- Is your organization effective?
- Do you consider your readers' knowledge and points of view?
- Do you represent yourself effectively?
- Do you conclude emphatically?

When you finish, make a list of your goals for the revision. You may have to write another draft before you move to the next stage.

7b REVISE WITH YOUR AUDIENCE AND PURPOSE IN MIND

1. **Keep your audience in mind.** Reread each paragraph's opening sentence and ask yourself whether the language is strong and engaging enough to keep your reader interested in your argument from paragraph to paragraph.
2. **Sharpen your focus wherever possible.** Revise your thesis and supporting paragraphs as needed. Check to see that your focus remains consistent throughout the essay.
3. **Check that key terms are adequately defined.** What are your key terms? Are they defined precisely enough to be meaningful?
4. **Develop where necessary.** Key points and claims may need more explanation and supporting evidence.
5. **Check links between paragraphs.** Underline the first and last sentences of each paragraph in your paper and then read these underlined sentences out loud to a friend. Do these sentences together make a logical and coherent argument?
6. **Consider your title.** Be as specific as you can in your title, and, if possible, suggest your stance.
7. **Consider your introduction.** In the introduction you want to get off to a fast start and convince your reader to keep reading.
8. **Consider your conclusion.** Try to leave your reader with something interesting and provocative.
9. **Improve the visual aspects of your text.** Does the font—the style and size of type—you selected look attractive? Do you use the same font throughout? Are you consistent if you use more than one font? Do you include headings and subheadings to identify key sections of your argument? Would illustrations or charts help to establish key points?

7c EDIT FOR SPECIFIC GOALS

1. **Check the connections between sentences.** If you need to signal the relationship from one sentence to the next, use a transitional word or phrase.

2. **Check your sentences.** If you noticed that a sentence was hard to read or didn't sound right when you read your paper aloud, think about how you might rephrase it.

3. **Eliminate wordiness.** See how many words you can take out without losing the meaning (see Chapter 19).

4. **Use active verbs.** Any time you can use a verb besides a form of *be* (*is, are, was, were*) or a verb ending in *-ing,* take advantage of the opportunity to make your style more lively.

5. **Use specific and inclusive language.** As you read, stay alert for any vague words or phrases. Check to make sure that you have used inclusive language throughout (see Chapter 21).

7d PROOFREAD CAREFULLY

1. **Know what your spelling checker can and can't do.** Spelling checkers do not catch wrong words (e.g., "to much" should be "too much"), missing endings ("three dog"), and other, similar errors.

2. **Check for grammar and mechanics.** Nothing hurts your credibility with readers more than a text with numerous errors.

CHAPTER 8

Designing and Presenting

8a DESIGN BASICS

Design is integral to the writing process. If you pay attention to design basics, your main points will be emphasized and readers will appreciate the look and the clarity of your presentation.

Christian Popolo
609 McCaslin Lane
Manitou Springs, CO 80829
719-555-0405
c.popolo@hotmail.com

OBJECTIVE
Production assistant position for an innovative Colorado television
program requiring prior experience in children's television and a strong
technical background.

EDUCATION
Bachelor of Arts in Communications, Boston College, May 2006
GPA: 3.65/4.0

WORK EXPERIENCE
Producer, *All the News,* BCTV Campus Television, Chestnut Hill, MA,
August 2003–May 2006. Produced a weekly, half-hour campus news
program. Supervised seven studio staffers and eight reporters.
Spearheaded successful initiative to increase Student Services funding
of the program by 15%.

Intern, *Zoom,* Boston, MA, May 2005–May 2006. Interned in the
production department of award-winning national children's television
program. Assisted in production of on-location shoots. Wrote and
produced three 2-minute "Hablamos" segments, designed to teach Span-
ish phrases.

Technician, Communications Media Lab, Chestnut Hill, MA, August
2002–April 2005. Maintained over $300,000 worth of the latest filming
and editing technology. Provided technical support for five to six
Communications courses each semester. Led monthly seminars for
undergraduates on the Avid nonlinear editing system.

FIGURE 8.1   The elements in this résumé are consistent, but there is not enough
visual contrast between what is more important and what is less important.

The first questions to ask when creating a design are

• What are the elements of the design?
• Which element is most important?

Christian Popolo

609 McCaslin Lane
Manitou Springs, CO 80829
719–555–0405
c.popolo@hotmail.com

OBJECTIVE

Production assistant position for an innovative Colorado
television program requiring prior experience in children's
television and a strong technical background.

EDUCATION

May 2006
   Bachelor of Arts in Communications, Boston College
   GPA: 3.65/4.0

EXPERIENCE

August 2003–May 2006
**Producer, *All the News*, BCTV Campus Television,
Chestnut Hill, MA**
         Produced a weekly, half-hour campus news program.
         Supervised seven studio staffers and eight reporters.
         Spearheaded successful initiative to increase Student
         Services funding of the program by 15%.

May 2005–May 2006
Intern, *Zoom*, Boston, MA
         Interned in the production department of award-winning
         national children's television program. Assisted in production
         of on-location shoots. Wrote and produced three 2-minute
         "Hablamos" segments, designed to teach Spanish phrases.

FIGURE 8.2   The revised résumé emphasizes relevant work experience. The design
directs the reader's attention to certain elements and creates a good impression.

The basic principles of good design

- Create visual relationships
- Make similar items look similar
- Make different items look different

8b   TABLES, CHARTS, AND GRAPHS

Word processing software makes it easy to create tables, charts, and graphs or to import them from other programs.

When to use tables

- To present a summary of several factors
- To present exact numbers
- To give an orderly arrangement so readers can locate and compare information

Name of item	Factor 1	Factor 2	Factor 3
AAA	000	00	0
BBB	00	0	000
CCC	0	000	00

When to use charts and graphs

- To direct readers to what is important
- To give evidence for claims
- To show factual information visually
- To show statistical relationships more clearly than either words or numbers alone permit

Selecting the right chart or graph

	Bar charts	Make comparisons in particular categories
	Line graphs	Show proportional trends over time
	Pie charts	Show the proportion of parts in terms of the whole
	Flowcharts	Show the steps in a process

PART TWO

Researching

9   PLANNING YOUR RESEARCH

a   Analyze the research task
b   Find a topic that interests you
c   Ask a question and draft a working thesis
d   Decide what kind of research you need to do

10   FINDING PRINT SOURCES IN LIBRARIES

a   Determine what kinds of sources you will need
b   Identify keywords
c   Find books
d   Find journal articles
e   Find newspaper articles
f   Start a working bibliography

11   FINDING SOURCES ONLINE

a   Database sources versus Web sources
b   Find articles and other sources in library databases
c   Find information on the Web
d   Find visual sources online

12   EVALUATING SOURCES

a   Determine the relevance of sources
b   Determine the reliability of print sources
c   Determine the reliability of Internet sources

13   USING SOURCES ETHICALLY AND EFFECTIVELY

a   Avoid plagiarism
b   Quote sources without plagiarizing
c   Summarize and paraphrase sources without plagiarizing
d   Incorporate quotations, summaries, and paraphrases effectively

CHAPTER 9
Planning Your Research

Research means both **investigating existing knowledge** that is stored on computers and in libraries, and **creating new knowledge** through original analysis, surveys, experiments, and theorizing. When you start a research task, you need to understand the different kinds of research and to plan your strategy in advance.

9a ANALYZE THE RESEARCH TASK

If you have an assignment that requires research, look closely at what you are being asked to do. The assignment may ask you to review, compare, survey, analyze, evaluate, or prove that something is true or untrue. The purpose of your research will help guide your strategies for research.

Determine your purpose

- An *analysis* or *examination* requires you to look at an issue in detail, explaining how it has evolved, who or what it affects, and what is at stake.
- A *review of scholarship* requires you to summarize what key scholars and researchers have written about the issue.
- A *survey* requires you to gather opinion about a particular issue, either by a questionnaire or by interviews.
- An *evaluation* requires you to make critical judgments.
- An *argument* requires you to assemble evidence in support of a claim you make.

Do you want to inform your readers, change their attitudes, or persuade them to take some action?

9b FIND A TOPIC THAT INTERESTS YOU

Ask meaningful questions and research will be enjoyable. Your courses may give you some ideas about questions to ask, or you may simply want to pursue an interest of your own.

Browse a Web subject directory

Several Web search sites (Britannica, LookSmart, and Yahoo! are some of the best known) include **subject directories**. Web directories are useful when you want to narrow a topic or learn what subcategories a topic might contain. The most popular subject directory, Yahoo! (www.yahoo.com), will retrieve both Web sites indexed by Yahoo! staff members and sites from the entire Web using **search engine** technology. In addition to the Web subject directories, the Library of Congress Virtual Reference Shelf (www.loc.gov/rr/askalib/virtualref.html) may help you identify sites relevant to your topic.

Consult general and specialized encyclopedias

General encyclopedias, which provide basic information about a wide range of topics, are also a good starting point for browsing. Two of the best known are the *Columbia Encyclopedia* (www.bartleby.com) and *Encyclopaedia Britannica* (www.eb.com).

Specialized encyclopedias focus on a single area of knowledge, go into more depth about a subject, and often include bibliographies. Your library may have handouts for specialized encyclopedias and other specialized reference sources, or you can consult Robert Balay's *Guide to Reference Books*, which should be available at the reference desk.

9c ASK A QUESTION AND DRAFT A WORKING THESIS

Often you'll be surprised by the amount of information your initial browsing uncovers. Your next task will be to identify in that mass of information a question for your research project. This **researchable question** to which you may want to formulate an initial answer, or **working thesis**, will be the focus of the remainder of your research and ultimately of your research project or paper (see Section 5b).

TOPIC Economic impacts of casino gambling

RESEARCH How does the presence of a casino affect the economy of
QUESTION the community where it is located?

| WORKING THESIS | The economic impact of casino gambling on the communities in which it is located is mixed, with some businesses benefiting and others suffering. |

9d DECIDE WHAT KIND OF RESEARCH YOU NEED TO DO

Once you have formulated a research question, you should begin thinking about what kind of research you will need to do to address the question.

Secondary research

Research based on the work of others is called **secondary research**. In the past this information was contained almost exclusively in collections of print materials housed in libraries, but today enormous amounts of information are available on the Internet and in various recorded media.

Primary research

Primary research includes experiments, data-gathering surveys and interviews, detailed observations, and the examination of historical documents. Primary research using personal observation, interviews, and surveys is also known as **field research**.

C H A P T E R   1 0

Finding Print Sources in Libraries

You may have heard people say that you can find any information you want on the Web. In fact, most books, films, recordings, scholarly journals, and older newspapers that you can find in a library are not on the Web. The resources in your library have been reviewed by librarians, so the quality is generally high and the materials are logically organized. Furthermore, when you go to the library, you have a librarian to help you if you cannot find what you are looking for.

10a DETERMINE WHAT KINDS OF SOURCES YOU WILL NEED

Before you begin your library research, you should determine what kinds of sources you will need.

Types of sources

Source	Type of Information	How to Find Them
Scholarly books (see pp. 37–38)	Extensive and in-depth coverage of nearly any subject	Library catalog
Scholarly journals (see pp. 38–40)	Reports of new knowledge and research findings written by experts	Print indexes and library databases
Trade journals (see pp. 38–40)	Reports of information pertaining to specific fields and products	Print indexes and library databases
Popular magazines (see pp. 38–40)	Reports or summaries of current news, sports, fashion, entertainment subjects	Print indexes and library databases
Newspapers (see pp. 40–41)	Recent and current information; foreign newspapers are useful for international perspectives	Print indexes and library databases
Government publications	Government-collected statistics, studies, and reports; especially good for science and medicine	Library catalog and city, state, and federal government Web sites
Videos, audios, documentaries, maps (see pp. 50–51)	Information varies widely	Library catalog Web sites

10b   IDENTIFY KEYWORDS

Your library catalog offers you two primary ways of searching. You can search by exact phrase, called **browse** searching. Or you can search by using **keywords**.

Browse searches

Browse searches allow you to search by author and title. You have to use the exact words.

- For authors: The name is inverted with the last name first. No comma is needed.

  Example: **Shakespeare William**

- For titles: The initial article (*a, an, the*) must be dropped.

  Example: **Merchant of Venice** *not* The Merchant of Venice. You can also search with the initial word or words of a title, e.g., **Merchant**.

Keyword searches

Keyword searches allow you to search all fields in the library's catalog. Furthermore, keyword searches are the primary way to find information in library databases (see Section 11b) and on the Web (see Section 11c).

Begin with your research question and working thesis.

Topic	Steroid use in high schools
Research question	How many high school athletes use steroids and what are the effects?
Working thesis	At a time when the percentage of <u>high school athletes</u> who use <u>steroids</u> is rapidly increasing, high schools must begin <u>testing</u> athletes to protect them from the many dangerous <u>effects of steroid use</u>.

Underline the key terms in your thesis. Then think of as many synonyms and related terms as you can and make lists.

HIGH SCHOOL ATHLETES	**TESTING**	**STEROIDS**	**EFFECTS OF STEROID USE**
teenage athletes	cost of testing	drugs	high blood pressure
high school students	cheating	drug abuse	liver damage
middle school students	cleansing urine	anabolic steroids	blood clots
adolescents	mandatory testing	roids	bowel problems
weight lifters	random testing	megadoses	urination problems
body image	testing for marijuana and cocaine	pyramiding	sleep problems
	legal supple-ments—DHEA, creatine, and andro	stacking testosterone	impotence in men
			menstrual problems in women
			rage and mood swings
			depression

When you have your keywords, use them to search your library's catalog. For example, if you do a keyword search using *high school students* and *steroids* as the keywords, you might find these words in the TITLE field or in the SUBJECT field; those in the TITLE field are highlighted below.

FULL DISPLAY

AUTHOR:
 Munro, Regina.
TITLE:
 Anabolic steroids : knowledge, attitude, and behavior in college age students / by Regina Munro.
PUBLISHED:
 1991.
DESCRIPTION:
 xii, 95 leaves.
NOTES:
 "UO 92 237--UO 92 238."
 Thesis (M.S.)--Arizona State University, 1991.
 Includes bibliographical references (leaves (88)-91).
 Microfiche. Eugene : Microform Publications, University of Oregon, 1992. 2 microfiches : negative.
SUBJECTS:
 Weight lifting--Psychological aspects.
 Anabolic steroids
 College students--Psychology
OCLC NUMBER:
 26885370

Locations:
MCFICHE 13,719 Microforms PCL Level 1 USE IN LIBRARY ONLY

10c FIND BOOKS

Scholarly books offer you in-depth analysis of many subjects. They also contain bibliographies that can help you find other resources on the particular subject.

Locating books in your library

A subject search for *attention deficit hyperactivity disorder* AND *adults* might turn up the following record in your library.

AUTHOR
Wender, Paul H., 1934-

TITLE
ADHD: attention-deficit hyperactivity disorder in children and adults

PUBLISHED
Oxford ; New York : Oxford University Press, 2000.

DESCRIPTION
ix, 277 p.; 22 cm.

NOTES
Includes index.

SUBJECTS
Attention-deficit hyperactivity disorder.
Attention-deficit disordered children.
Attention-deficit disordered adults.

OCLC NUMBER
44118022
Locations
RJ 506 H9 W448 2000 Main Library Stacks

The floors of your library where books are shelved are referred to as the *stacks*. The call number will enable you to find the item in the stacks. The locations guide for your library will give the level and section.

10d FIND JOURNAL ARTICLES

Like books, **scholarly journals** provide in-depth examinations of subjects. The articles in scholarly journals are written by experts, and they usually contain lists of references that can guide you to other research on a subject. Articles in **trade and popular journals** and magazines are typically written by journalists. **Popular magazines** are useful for gaining general information.

Indexes for scholarly journals and magazines are located in the reference area of your library, and many may also be available on your library's Web site. Online indexes are databases, fully searchable by author, title, subject, or keywords, and they are often referred to as *databases* instead of *indexes* (see Section 11b).

Your library has a list of databases and indexes by subject. Find this subject index either on your library's Web site or in the reference section of your library.

General indexes and databases

These indexes include thousands of publications from many fields. They will give you either the full text of a publication or an abstract—a short summary of the contents. For more on how to use full-text databases, see Section 11b.

- **Academic Search Premier** (EBSCO). Provides full text for over 3,000 scholarly publications, including social sciences, humanities, education, computer sciences, engineering, language and linguistics, literature, medical sciences, and ethnic studies journals.
- **ArticleFirst** (FirstSearch). Indexes over 15,000 journals in business, the humanities, medicine, science, and social sciences.
- **Biography and Genealogy Master Index** (Thompson Gale). Indexes biographies, autobiographies, and interviews for over four million people.

- **Expanded Academic ASAP** (Thompson Gale). Indexes 2,300 periodicals from the arts, humanities, sciences, social sciences, and general news, some with full-text articles available.
- **Factiva** (Dow Jones). Gives full-text access to major newspapers, market research reports, and business journals, including *The Wall Street Journal.*
- **Ingenta.com** (Ingenta). Gives citations to over 20,000 multidisciplinary journals.
- **LexisNexis Academic** (LexisNexis). Provides full text of a wide range of newspapers, magazines, government and legal documents, and company profiles from around the world.
- **WorldCat** (FirstSearch). Contains over 52 million records of books and other materials in libraries throughout the world but very few articles in journals.

Specialized indexes and databases

In addition, many specialized indexes list citations to journal articles in various fields. While some are full-text databases, most will give you abstracts of publications. Some of the more important are the following.

- **Business and Company Resource Center** (Thompson Gale). Provides access to company profiles, investment reports, company histories, and periodicals.
- **Business Source Premier** (EBSCO). Indexes and provides abstracts for articles in scholarly journals in accounting, economics, finance, management, and international business.
- **CINAHL** (EBSCO, Ovid). The Cumulative Index to Nursing & Allied Health (CINAHL) database indexes books and nearly a thousand journals related to nursing and allied health disciplines.
- **ERIC** (EBSCO, FirstSearch). Indexes journal articles, technical reports, curricular materials, and other publications in education.
- **GeoRef** (COS, EBSCO). Indexes books, journal articles, conference papers, maps, dissertations, and other publications related to geology and geoscience.

- **MEDLINE** (EBSCO, FirstSearch, Ovid). Primary index and source for abstracts of publications and journals related to medicine and health care.
- **MLA International Bibliography** (EBSCO, Ovid). Indexes books and articles about literature in English and other languages, folklore, linguistics, drama, and rhetoric and writing.
- **PsychINFO** (EBSCO, Ovid). Covers thoroughly the discipline of psychology, but also has many items from business, education, law, linguistics, medicine, sociology, and other related disciplines.
- **SciFinder Scholar** (ACS). Offers easy-to-use and comprehensive coverage of chemistry from the American Chemical Society. Also accesses MedLine.
- **Web of Science** (ISI). Provides Web access to all three ISI citation indexes—Arts & Humanities Citation Index, Science Citation Index Expanded, and Social Sciences Citation Index.

10e FIND NEWSPAPER ARTICLES

Newspaper articles are a valuable resource, especially on local topics that aren't covered by other sources and on very recent topics. You can also read newspaper articles from the past to learn how people understood events as they happened. Newspaper articles can be located in indexes similar to those for journals. For issues more than a few years old, you will likely have to read the newspaper on microfilm.

Online newspaper collections

For current topics you can now find many newspaper articles online. Check your library's Web page to find out if your library subscribes to these important online collections, which give you access to hundreds of newspapers.

- **Factiva** (Dow Jones). Gives full-text access to major newspapers with a business orientation.
- **InfoTrac Newspapers** (Thompson Gale). Offers full-text access to over 100 newspapers.

- **LexisNexis Academic** (LexisNexis). Provides full-text access to international, national, and regional newspapers.
- **Newspaper Source** (EBSCO). Gives full-text access to leading national and international newspapers and over 200 regional newspapers.

Links to newspaper sites

Nearly every major newspaper now allows you to read current articles online. Be aware, however, that what you find one day may not be available without charge when you return to the newspaper's Web site. You can find links to hundreds of newspapers on these sites.

- **News and Newspapers Online** (library.uncg.edu/news/). Offers links to U.S. and foreign newspapers.
- **NewsLink** (newslink.org). Gives links to newspapers, magazines, and radio and TV stations in the United States and other countries.
- **News Voyager** (www.newspaperlinks.com). Provides links to U.S. and Canadian newspaper sites, as well as selected links to international newspapers.
- **CollegeNews.com** (www.collegenews.com). Search tool for finding student-run and campus newspapers.

Many newspapers now make some past issues available online for a fee. The most comprehensive directory of online newspaper archives is *U.S. News Archives on the Web* (www.ibiblio.org/slanews/internet/archives.html).

10f START A WORKING BIBLIOGRAPHY

As you begin to collect your sources, make sure you get full bibliographic information for everything you might want to use in your project: articles, books, Web sites, and other materials.

Necessary bibliographic information

For books you will need, at minimum, the following information. This information can typically be found on the front and back of the title page:

- Author's name
- Title of the book
- Place of publication
- Name of publisher
- Date of publication

You will also need the page numbers if you are quoting directly or referring to a specific passage, and the title and author of the individual chapter if your source is an edited book with contributions by several people.

For journals you will need

- Author's name
- Title of the article
- Title of the journal
- Volume and issue of the journal
- Date of the issue
- Page numbers of the article

Visual and multimedia sources vary widely, but you should try to capture as many of the following types of information as you can find:

- Artist's or author's name
- Title of the work
- Date the work was created
- Location of the work (e.g., archive, gallery, museum)
- Medium or media in which the work appears (e.g., DVD, poster, cartoon)
- Page or figure number (if the source comes from a printed book)

In general, as you research and develop a working bibliography, write down more information rather than less. It is time-consuming to go back later to sources to find missing bibliographic information.

C H A P T E R   1 1
Finding Sources Online

Many colleges and universities have made most of the major resources in their reference rooms available online. Newspapers, scholarly journals, and government documents are increasingly being published and archived in digital form. Knowing how to use library databases gives you access to vast quantities of information that can be delivered to your computer.

11a DATABASE SOURCES VERSUS WEB SOURCES

There is a world of difference between doing a search on library databases through your library's Web site and doing a general search on the Web using Google. Library databases have the advantages of high quality and no commercial intrusion along with the convenience of Web delivery. When you search a subject on Google, the results often give you a series of commercial sites selling books and products related to the words you typed in. (See the chart on page 44.)

11b FIND ARTICLES AND OTHER SOURCES IN LIBRARY DATABASES

Find databases

Usually you can find databases on your library's Web site. Sometimes you will find a list of databases. Sometimes you select a subject, and then you are directed to databases.

Use databases

You will need keywords to search in a database. Your next decision is to choose a database to begin your research.

Advantages	Library database sources	Web sources
Speed—find information quickly	✓	✓
Accessible—available 24/7	✓	✓
Organized—materials are organized for efficient search and retrieval	✓	
High quality—librarians review and select the resources	✓	
Comprehensive—librarians review and select the resources	✓	
Permanent—library materials remain available for many years	✓	

Disadvantages	Library database sources	Web sources
Biased—often the soapbox for organizations		✓
Commercial—often trying to sell you something		✓
Lack permanence—here today, gone tomorrow		✓
Uneven quality—anyone can put up a Web site		✓

Academic Search Premier is a good general database to research current topics. You can find Academic Search Premier either on a list of databases or under EBSCOhost on your library's Web site. If you wish to get only full-text articles, you can check that option (see Figure 11.1). Full-text documents give you the same text you would find in print.

Another major database for researching current issues is LexisNexis Academic, which allows you to limit a search by the kind of publication and by date. For example, the results of a search for *steroids* and *high school* are shown in Figure 11.2. Often you can determine by the title of the article if it is relevant to your topic.

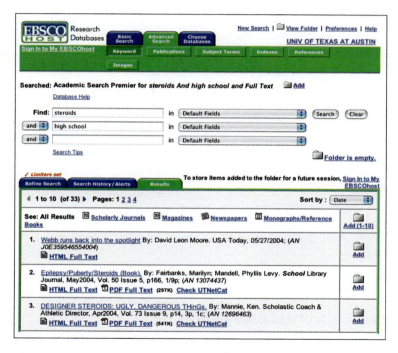

FIGURE 11.1 Results of a full-text search for *steroids* and *high school* on Academic Search Premier

11b Finding Sources Online

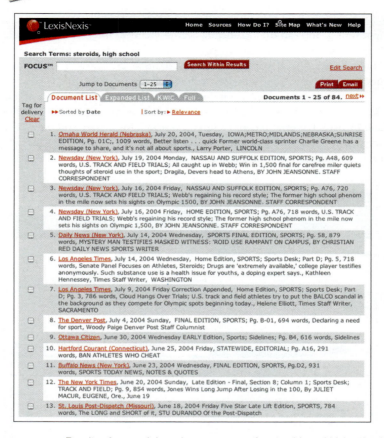

FIGURE 11.2 Results of a search in major newspapers for *steroids* and *high school* on LexisNexis Academic

Keep track of database sources

You must document information you get from database sources just as for print sources. Figure 11.3 shows an example of an article from the LexisNexis Academic search for *steroids* and *high school*. To cite this article

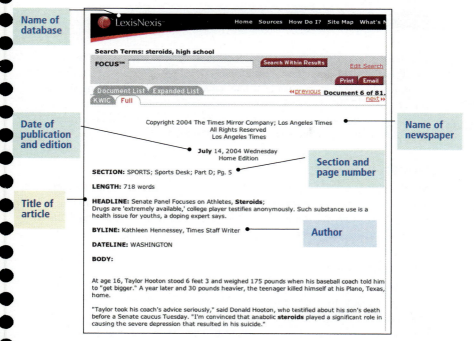

Name of database

Date of publication and edition

Title of article

Name of newspaper

Section and page number

Author

FIGURE 11.3 Citing a database article from LexisNexis Academic

in both MLA (see Chapter 14) and APA (see Chapter 15) styles, you'll
need the following information:

- Author
- Title of article
- Name of periodical
- Date of publication (and edition for newspapers)
- Section and page number
- Name of database
- Date of access (the day you found the article in the database)

11c FIND INFORMATION ON THE WEB

Because anyone can publish on the Web, there is no overall quality control and there is no system of organization, as there is in a library. Nevertheless, the Web offers you some resources for current topics that would be difficult or impossible to find in a library. The keys to success are knowing where you are most likely to find current and accurate information about the particular question you are researching, knowing how to access that information, and knowing how to test its reliability (see Chapter 12).

Search engines

Search engines designed for the Web work in ways similar to library databases and your library's online catalog but with one major difference. Databases typically do some screening of the items they list, but search engines potentially take you to everything on the Web—millions of pages in all.

Advanced searches

The advanced searches on Google and Yahoo! give you the options of using a string of words to search for sites that contain (1) all the words, (2) the exact phrase, (3) any of the words, (4) without certain words. They also allow you to specify the language of the site, the date range, the file format, and the domain. For example, if you want to limit a search for ADHD to government Web sites such as the National Institutes of Health, you can specify the domain as .gov (see Figure 11.4, opposite).

Tips for Web searches

Help! My search turned up too many results.
- Try more specific search terms.
- Combine the words with AND.
- Use a phrase within quotation marks or specify "the exact phrase."
- Specify NOT for terms you are not interested in finding.
- Limit the search by a date range.

Help! My search turned up too few results.
- Check your spelling.
- Try broader search terms.
- Use OR instead of AND, or specify "find any of the words."
- Try another index or search engine.

Archives

An archive is traditionally a physical place where historical documents, such as manuscripts and letters, are stored. Recently the term has come to mean any collection of documents, typically preserved for educational purposes. All archives focus on preserving materials for posterity. Given the rapidly changing nature of the Web, electronic archives strive to preserve access to their materials. One especially useful archive is the American Memory collection, containing verbal and visual texts documenting U.S. history (memory.loc.gov/ammem/).

FIGURE 11.4 Yahoo! advanced search for ADHD excluding children and limiting the domain to .gov

Keep track of Web research

You will need the following information to document sources you find on the Web.

- Name of the page
- Author if listed
- Sponsoring organization if listed
- Date the site was posted
- Date you visited
- Complete URL

See Section 14g for detailed instructions on how to find the information you need for MLA documentation. See Section 15e for instructions on finding the information you need for APA documentation.

11d FIND VISUAL SOURCES ONLINE

Visual databases and the Web give you access to many visual sources that were difficult to locate just a few years ago.

Visual databases

Several libraries have made large collections of photographs and other visual materials available on their Web sites. Major image resources are also available from U.S. government Web sites, including space exploration images from NASA, medical images from NIH, and historical images from the Library of Congress.

Visual sources on the Web

Millions of images have been published on the Web, and you can search for them using Google and other search engines that allow you to specify searches for images. Some search engines such as Ditto (www.ditto.com) are designed specifically to find images. Yahoo! Picture Gallery has over 400,000 images that can be searched by subject (gallery.yahoo.com). In addition to images, you can find statistical data represented in charts and graphs on government Web sites. Especially useful is the Statistical Abstract of the United States for finding charts and graphs of population statistics (www.census.gov/statab/www/). You can also find thousands of maps on the Web (see www.lib.utexas.edu/maps/map_sites/map_sites.html for a directory of map sites).

Downloading and inserting images

You will need the following information to document visual sources you find on the Web.

- Title of the work
- Author or artist
- Name of the site or archive
- Sponsoring organization if listed
- Date the site was posted
- Date you visited
- Complete URL

Just because images are easy to download from the Web does not mean that every image is available for you to use. Look for the image creator's copyright notice and suggested credit line. This notice will tell you if you can reproduce the image. Most images on government Web sites can be reproduced, but check the copyright restrictions. You should acknowledge the source of any image you use.

Using visuals in a research paper

Here are a few guidelines to keep in mind for incorporating visual sources into your research paper.

- **Use visuals for examples and supporting evidence, not for decoration.**
- **Refer to images and other graphics in the body of your research paper.** Explain in the body of your paper the significance of any image or graphic.
- **Include captions for images and other graphics.**
- **Respect the copyright of visual sources.** You may need to request permission to use a visual from the Web. Use public domain material whenever possible.
- **Get complete citation information.** You are required to cite visual sources in your list of works cited just as you are required to cite other sources.

CHAPTER 12

Evaluating Sources

Becoming a successful researcher requires that you take a critical view of all sources you find. Learn to *evaluate* potential sources.

12a DETERMINE THE RELEVANCE OF SOURCES

A successful search will turn up many more items than you can expect to use in your final product. Return to your research question and working thesis (Section 9c). Use your research question and working thesis to make decisions about which sources are most relevant to your purpose.

Guidelines for determining the relevance of your sources

- Does your research question require you to consult primary or secondary sources?
- Does a source you have found address your question?
- Does a source support or disagree with your working thesis? (You should not throw out work that challenges your views.)
- Does a source add to your content in an important way?
- Is the material you have found persuasive?
- What indications of possible bias do you note in the source?

12b DETERMINE THE RELIABILITY OF PRINT SOURCES

Print sources contain their share of biased, inaccurate, and misleading information. But because books are expensive to print and distribute, book publishers generally protect their investment by providing some level of editorial oversight. Print sources in libraries have an additional layer of oversight because someone has decided that a book or journal is worth purchasing and cataloging.

Traditional criteria for evaluating print sources

- **Source.** Who published the book or article? Scholarly books and articles in scholarly journals are generally more reliable than popular magazines and books, which tend to emphasize what is sensational or entertaining at the expense of accuracy and comprehensiveness.
- **Author.** Who wrote the book or article? What are the author's qualifications?
- **Timeliness.** How current is the source? If you are researching a fast-developing subject such as treating ADHD, then currency is very important.
- **Evidence.** Where does the evidence come from—facts, interviews, observations, surveys, or experiments? Is the evidence adequate to support the author's claims?
- **Biases.** Can you detect particular biases of the author? How do the author's biases affect the interpretation offered?
- **Advertising.** Is advertising a prominent part of the journal or newspaper? How might the ads affect what gets printed?

12c DETERMINE THE RELIABILITY OF INTERNET SOURCES

Always approach Web sites with an eye toward evaluating content. Use the following questions to evaluate any Web site you are considering as a potential source.

A checklist for evaluating Web sources

- **What organization sponsors or pays for the Web site?** If the name of the organization is not given, determine what you can from the URL.

(continued next page)

- **Is the author of the Web site identified?** Can you get in touch with the author? Be cautious of information on an anonymous site.
- **Are the author's credentials listed on the Web site?** If the credentials are listed, are they relevant to the subject?
- **Is the information on the Web site current?** Can you discover when the Web site was last updated?
- **Are references provided for information given on the site?** References give you one way to check the validity of the information on the site.
- **Are there links to additional information?** Do the links work? Is the linked information reliable?
- **Does the Web site present balanced information or does it chiefly present one point of view?** Many Web sites appear to be balanced but neglect other points of view.
- **Is the Web site an advertisement for a product or service?** Many so-called informative Web sites are trying to sell you something.

You should be prepared to look at every Web site closely. For example, the Web site "The Fraud of Child Psychiatry" (see Figure 12.1) includes a list of MDs as authorities. But an examination of the site reveals that it is designed to sell books that take strong positions against psychotherapeutic drugs such as Prozac, Xanax, and Ritalin. The URL (www.outlookcities .com/children/), which has a .com suffix rather than .edu, .gov, or .org, tells you that this site is on a commercial server, not an institutional server. It could have been put up by anyone. A more reliable source on this topic might be the National Institute of Mental Health's ADHD page, located by a keyword search (www.nimh.nih.gov/publicat/adhd.html).

The Fraud of Child Psychiatry, ADD/ADHD, Attention Deficit Disorder, and Ritalin.

"...This elementary fact makes the child psychiatrist one of the most dangerous enemies not only of children, but also of adults who care for the two precious and most vulnerable things in life - children and liberty. Child psychology and child psychiatry cannot be reformed. They must be abolished." - Thomas Szasz M.D., *Cruel Compassion.*

"The pediatrician's wanton prescription of powerful drugs indoctrinates children from birth with the philosophy of 'a pill for every ill'."... "Doctors are directly responsible for hooking millions of people on prescription drugs. They are also indirectly responsible for the plight of millions more who turn to illegal drugs because they were taught at an early age that drugs can cure anything - including psychological and emotional conditions - that ails them. " - Robert S. Mendelsohn, M.D., *How to Raise a Healthy Child...In Spite of Your Doctor.*

Fred A. Baughman, M.D. - Immunize Your Child Against ADD

Ann B. Tracy, PhD - Psychiatric Drugs

Fred A. Baughman, M.D. - What You Should Know About ADD

If You Need Help

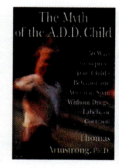

The Myth of the A.D.D. Child, by Thomas Armstrong, Ph.D.

The Myth of the A.D.D. Child exposes the mislabeling of millions of children as A.D.D./ A.D.H.D., and the use of powerful mind-altering drugs such as Ritalin in treating children's hyperactivity. Not long ago, children who behaved in certain ways were called "bundles of energy", "daydreamers," or "fireballs." Now they're considered "hyperactive," "distractible," or "impulsive"-victims of the ubiquitous Attention Deficit Disorder. Tragically, such labeling can follow a child through life. Worse, the mind-altering drugs prescribed for A.D.D./A.D.H.D. are unnecessary-and they are harmful.

FIGURE 12.1   Fraud of Child Psychiatry site (www.outlookcities.com/children/)

C H A P T E R   1 3

Using Sources Ethically and Effectively

Careful documentation of sources is essential to developing knowledge and allows scholars and researchers to build on the work of other scholars and researchers.

13a   AVOID PLAGIARISM

You know that copying someone else's paper word for word or taking an article off the Internet and turning it in as yours is plagiarism. But if plagiarism also means using the ideas, melodies, or images of someone else without acknowledging them, then the concept is much broader and more difficult to define.

What you don't have to document

Fortunately, common sense governs issues of academic plagiarism. The standards of documentation are not so strict that the source of every fact you cite must be acknowledged. Suppose you are writing about the causes of maritime disasters and you want to know how many people drowned when the *Titanic* sank on the early morning of April 15, 1912. You check the *Britannica Online* Web site and find that the death toll was around 1,500. Since this fact is available in many reference works, you would not need to cite *Britannica Online* as the source.

What you do have to document

For facts that are not easily found in general reference works, statements of opinion, and arguable claims, you should cite the source. You should also cite the sources of statistics, research findings, examples, graphs, charts, and illustrations. When in doubt, always document the source.

COMMON ERRORS

Plagiarism in college writing

If you find any of the following problems in your academic writing, it is likely you are plagiarizing someone else's work. Because plagiarism is usually inadvertent, it is especially important that you understand what constitutes using sources responsibly.

- **Missing attribution.** The author of a quotation has not been identified. A lead-in or signal phrase that provides attribution to the source is not used, and no author is identified in the citation.
- **Missing quotation marks.** Quotation marks do not appear around material quoted directly from a source.
- **Inadequate citation.** No page number is given to show where in the source the quotation, paraphrase, or summary is drawn from.
- **Paraphrase relies too heavily on the source.** Either the wording or sentence structure of a paraphrase follows the source too closely.
- **Distortion of meaning.** A paraphrase or summary distorts the meaning of the source, or a quotation is taken out of context, resulting in a change of meaning.
- **Missing Works Cited entry.** The Works Cited page does not include all the works cited in the paper.
- **Inadequate citation of images.** A figure or photo appears with no label, number, caption, or citation to indicate the source of the image. If material includes a summary of data from a visual source, no attribution or citation is given for the graph being summarized.

13b QUOTE SOURCES WITHOUT PLAGIARIZING

Most people who get into plagiarism trouble lift words from a source and use them without quotation marks. Where the line is drawn is easiest to illustrate with an example. In the following passage, Steven Johnson takes issue with the metaphor of surfing applied to the Web:

> Web surfing and channel surfing are genuinely different pursuits; to imagine them as equivalents is to ignore the defining characteristics of each medium. . . . A channel surfer hops back and forth between different channels because she's bored. A Web surfer clicks on a link because she's interested.
>
> —Johnson, Steven. *Interface Culture: How New Technology Transforms the Way We Create and Communicate.* New York: Harper, 1997. 107-09.

If you were writing a paper or putting up a Web site that concerned Web surfing, you might want to mention the distinction that Johnson makes between channel surfing and surfing on the Web. Your options are to paraphrase the source or to quote it directly.

If you quote directly, you must place quotation marks around all words you take from the original:

> One observer marks this contrast: "A channel surfer hops back and forth between different channels because she's bored. A Web surfer clicks on a link because she's interested" (Johnson 109).

Notice that the quotation is introduced and not just dropped in. This example follows Modern Language Association (MLA) style, where the citation goes outside the quotation marks but before the final period.

13c   SUMMARIZE AND PARAPHRASE SOURCES WITHOUT PLAGIARIZING

Summarize

When you *summarize,* you state the major ideas of an entire source or part of a source in a paragraph or perhaps even a sentence. The key is to put the summary in your own words. If you use words from the source, you have to put those words in quotation marks.

PLAGIARIZED

Steven Johnson argues in *Interface Culture* that the concept of "surfing" is misapplied to the Internet because channel surfers hop back and forth between different channels because they're bored, but Web surfers click on links because they're interested.

[Most of the words are lifted directly from the original.]

ACCEPTABLE SUMMARY
Steven Johnson argues in *Interface Culture* that the concept of "surfing" is misapplied to the Internet because users of the Web consciously choose to link to other sites while television viewers mindlessly flip through the channels until something catches their attention.

Paraphrase

When you *paraphrase,* you represent the idea of the source in your own words at about the same length as the original. You still need to include the reference to the source of the idea. The following example illustrates what is not an acceptable paraphrase.

PLAGIARIZED
Steven Johnson argues that the concept of "surfing" does a terrible injustice to what it means to navigate around the Web. What makes the idea of Web surfing infuriating is the association with television. Surfing is not a bad metaphor for channel hopping, but it doesn't fit what people do on the Web. Web surfing and channel surfing are truly different activities; to imagine them as the same is to ignore their defining characteristics. A channel surfer skips around because she's bored while a Web surfer clicks on a link because she's interested (107-09).

Even though the source is listed, this paraphrase is unacceptable. Too many of the words in the original are used directly here, including much or all of entire sentences. When a string of words is lifted from a source and inserted without quotation marks, the passage is plagiarized.

A true paraphrase represents an entire rewriting of the idea from the source.

ACCEPTABLE PARAPHRASE
Steven Johnson argues that "surfing" is a misleading term for describing how people navigate on the Web. He allows that "surfing" is appropriate for clicking across television channels because the viewer

has to interact with what the networks and cable companies provide, just as the surfer has to interact with what the ocean provides. Web surfing, according to Johnson, operates at much greater depth and with much more consciousness of purpose. Web surfers actively follow links to make connections (107-09).

Even though there are a few words from the original in this paraphrase, such as *navigate* and *connections*, these sentences are original in structure and wording while accurately conveying the meaning of the source.

13d INCORPORATE QUOTATIONS, SUMMARIES, AND PARAPHRASES EFFECTIVELY

The purpose of using sources is to *support* what you have to say, not to say it for you. Next to plagiarism, the worst mistake you can make with sources is to string together a series of long quotations. This strategy leaves your readers wondering whether you have anything to say. If you want to refer to an idea or fact and the original wording is not critical, make the point in your own words. Save direct quotations for language that is memorable or gives the character of the source.

Block quotations

If a direct quotation is long, it is indented from the margin instead of being placed in quotation marks. In MLA style, a quotation longer than four lines should be indented ten spaces. A quotation of forty words or longer is indented five spaces in APA style. In both MLA and APA styles, long quotations are double-spaced. When you indent a long quotation this way, it is called a **block quotation**. You still need to integrate a block quotation into the text of your paper. Block quotations should be introduced by mentioning where they came from. Note three points about form in the block quotation.

- There are no quotation marks around the block quotation.
- Words quoted in the original retain the double quotation marks.
- The page number appears after the period at the end of the block quotation.

It is a good idea to include at least one or two sentences following the quotation to describe its significance to your thesis.

Integrate quotations, summaries, and paraphrases

You should check to see whether all sources are well integrated into the fabric of your paper. Introduce quotations by attributing them in the text:

> Many soldiers who fought for the United States in the U.S.-Mexican War of 1846 were skeptical of American motives, including Civil War hero and future president Ulysses S. Grant, who wrote: "We were sent to provoke a fight, but it was essential that Mexico should commence it" (68).

Summaries and paraphrases likewise need introductions. In the following summary signal phrases make it clear which ideas come from the source. The summary also indicates the stance of Lewis and includes a short quotation that gives the flavor of the source.

> In 2001 it became as fashionable to say the Internet changes nothing as it had been to claim the Internet changes everything just two years before. In the midst of the Internet gloom, one prominent contrarian has emerged to defend the Internet. Michael Lewis observes in *Next: The Future Just Happened* that it's as if "some crusty old baron who had been blasted out of his castle and was finally having a look at his first cannon had said, 'All it does is speed up balls'" (14). Lewis claims that while the profit-making potential of the Internet was overrated, the social effects were not. He sees the Internet demolishing old castles of expertise along with many traditional relationships based on that expertise.

Use quotations effectively

Quotations are a frequent problem area in research papers. Review every quotation to ensure that each is used effectively and correctly.

- **Limit the use of long quotations.** If you have more than one block quotation on a page, look closely to see if one or more can be paraphrased or summarized. *(continued next page)*

14 MLA DOCUMENTATION

a The elements of MLA documentation
b Sample in-text citations
c Books
d Journals and magazines
e Newspapers
f Government documents, pamphlets, dissertations, and letters
g Online publications
h CD-ROM, software, and unedited online sources
i Visual sources
j Multimedia sources
k Sample research paper and works-cited pages

15 APA DOCUMENTATION

a The elements of APA documentation
b Sample in-text citations
c Books and nonperiodical sources
d Periodical sources
e Online sources
f Visual, computer, and multimedia sources
g Sample research paper and reference pages

16 CMS DOCUMENTATION

a The elements of CMS documentation
b Books and nonperiodical sources
c Periodical sources
d Online and computer sources
e Sample research paper and bibliography pages

17 CSE DOCUMENTATION

a The elements of CSE documentation
b In-text citations
c Books and nonperiodical sources
d Periodical sources
e Online sources

CHAPTER 14

MLA Documentation

The Modern Language Association (MLA) style is the documentation style used in the humanities and fine arts. If you have questions that this chapter does not address, consult the *MLA Handbook for Writers of Research Papers,* sixth edition (2003), and the *MLA Style Manual and Guide to Scholarly Publishing,* second edition (1998).

14a THE ELEMENTS OF MLA DOCUMENTATION

In-text citations

Quotations, summaries, and paraphrases from outside sources are indicated by in-text citations in parentheses. When readers find a parenthetical reference in the body of a paper, they can turn to the works-cited list at the end of the paper to find complete publication information for the cited source.

Describing humans as "innate mind readers," one observer argues that "our skill at imagining other people's mental states ranks up there with our knack for language and our opposable thumbs" (Johnson 196).

Works Cited

Johnson, Steven. Emergence: The Connected Lives of Ants, Brains, Cities, and Software. New York: Scribner, 2001.

The works-cited list

The works-cited list is organized alphabetically by authors' last names. (See Section 14k, pages 99–100, for a sample works-cited list.)

14b **SAMPLE IN-TEXT CITATIONS IN MLA STYLE**

1. Author named in your text

Put the author's name in a signal phrase in your sentence.

Sociologist Daniel Bell called this emerging U.S. economy the
"postindustrial society" (3).

2. Author not named in your text

In 1997, the Gallup poll reported that 55% of adults in the United
States think secondhand smoke is "very harmful," compared to only
36% in 1994 (Saad 4).

3. Work by one author

The author's last name comes first, followed by the page number.
There is no comma.

(Bell 3)

4. Work by two or three authors

The authors' last names follow the order of the title page. If there are
two authors, join the names with *and*. If there are three, use commas between the first two names and a comma with *and* before the last name.

(Francisco, Vaughn, and Lynn 7)

5. Work by four or more authors

You may use the phrase *et al.* (meaning "and others") for all names but
the first, or you may write out all the names. Make sure you use the same
method for both the in-text citations and the works-cited list.

(Abrams et al. 1653)

6. Work by an unnamed author

Use a shortened version of the title that includes at least the first important word.

> A review in The New Yorker of Ryan Adams's new album focuses on the artist's age ("Pure" 25).

"Pure" is in quotation marks because it refers to the title of an article.

7. Work by a group or organization

Treat the group or organization as the author. Identify the group author in the text and place only the page number in the parentheses.

> According to the Irish Free State Handbook, published by the Ministry for Industry and Finance, the population of Ireland in 1929 was approximately 4,192,000 (23).

8. Quotations longer than four lines

NOTE: When using indented ("block") quotations longer than four lines, the period appears *before* the parentheses enclosing the page number.

> In her article "Art for Everybody," Susan Orlean attempts to explain the popularity of painter Thomas Kinkade:
>
> > People like to own things they think are valuable. . . . The high price of limited editions is part of their appeal: it implies that they are choice and exclusive, and that only a certain class of people will be able to afford them. (128)
>
> This same statement could possibly also explain the popularity of phenomena like PBS's Antiques Road Show.

If the source is longer than one page, provide the page number for each quotation, paraphrase, and summary.

9. Online and multimedia sources

See Section 14g for further information on citing Web sites and other online sources. Because many online sources do not include page numbers, they are usually named in text rather than in a parenthetical citation.

In a hypertext version of James Joyce's <u>Ulysses</u>, . . .

If an online source includes paragraph numbers rather than page numbers, use *par.* with the number.

(Cello, par. 4)

Multimedia sources (music, film, DVDs, TV programs, interviews) are also usually named in text rather than in a parenthetical citation.

<u>House of Flying Daggers</u> was one of the first feature films to be released on Sony's UMD format for the PSP portable system.

10. Work in an anthology

Cite the name of the author of the work within an anthology, not the name of the editor of the collection. Alphabetize the entry in the list of works cited by the author, not the editor.

In "Beard," Melissa Jane Hardie explores the role assumed by Elizabeth Taylor as the celebrity companion of gay actors including Rock Hudson and Montgomery Cliff (278-79).

11. Two or more works by the same author

Use the author's last name and then a shortened version of the title of each source.

The majority of books written about coauthorship focus on partners of the same sex (Laird, <u>Women</u> 351).

Note that *Women* is underlined because it is the name of a book; if an article were named, quotation marks would be used.

12. Different authors with the same last name

Include the initial of the author's first name in the parenthetical reference.

Web surfing requires more mental involvement than channel surfing
(S. Johnson 107).

13. Two or more sources within the same sentence

Place each citation directly after the statement it supports.

Many sweeping pronouncements were made in the 1990s that the
Internet is the best opportunity to improve education since the
printing press (Ellsworth xxii) or even in the history of the world
(Dyrli and Kinnaman 79).

14. Two or more sources within the same citation

If two sources support a single point, separate them with a semicolon.

(McKibbin 39; Gore 92)

15. Work quoted in another source

National governments have become increasingly what Ulrich Beck, in
a 1999 interview, calls "zombie institutions"—institutions which are
"dead and still alive" (qtd. in Bauman 6).

16. Literary works

To supply a reference to literary works, you sometimes need more than
a page number from a specific edition. Readers should be able to locate a
quotation in any edition of the book. Give the page number from the edition that you are using, then a semicolon and other identifying information.

"Marriage is a house" is one of the most memorable lines in Don
Quixote (546; pt. 2, bk. 3, ch. 19).

14c BOOKS IN MLA-STYLE WORKS CITED

TITLE PAGE

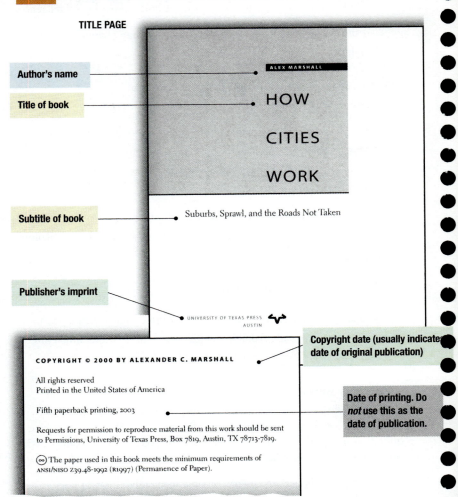

Author's name — ALEX MARSHALL

Title of book — HOW CITIES WORK

Subtitle of book — Suburbs, Sprawl, and the Roads Not Taken

Publisher's imprint — UNIVERSITY OF TEXAS PRESS
AUSTIN

COPYRIGHT © 2000 BY ALEXANDER C. MARSHALL

All rights reserved
Printed in the United States of America

Fifth paperback printing, 2003

Requests for permission to reproduce material from this work should be sent to Permissions, University of Texas Press, Box 7819, Austin, TX 78713-7819.

∞ The paper used in this book meets the minimum requirements of ANSI/NISO Z39.48-1992 (R1997) (Permanence of Paper).

Copyright date (usually indicates date of original publication)

Date of printing. Do *not* use this as the date of publication.

DETAIL OF COPYRIGHT PAGE

Marshall, Alex. How Cities Work: Suburbs, Sprawl, and the Roads Not Taken. Austin: U of Texas P, 2000.

AUTHOR'S OR EDITOR'S NAME

The author's last name comes first, followed by a comma and the first name.

For edited books, put the abbreviation *ed.* after the name, preceded by a comma:

Kavanagh, Peter, ed.

BOOK TITLE

Use the exact title, as it appears on the title page (not the cover).

Underline the title.

All nouns, verbs, pronouns, adjectives, adverbs, and subordinating conjunctions, and the first word of the title are capitalized. Do not capitalize articles, preposi- tions, coordinating con- junctions, or *to* infinitives, unless they are the first word of the title.

PUBLICATION INFORMATION

Place of publication

If more than one city is given, use the first.

For cities outside the U.S. add an abbreviation of the country or province if the city is not well known.

Publisher

Use a short form of the name:

Omit words such as *Press, Publisher,* and *Inc.*

For university presses, use *UP*: New York UP

Shorten the name. For example, shorten *Addison, Wesley, Longman* to *Longman; W. W. Norton & Co.* to *Norton.*

Date of publication

Give the year as it appears on the copyright page.

If no year of publication is given, but can be approximated, put a *c.* ("circa") and the approximate date in brackets: [c. 1999].

Otherwise, put *n.d.* ("no date"): Cambridge: Harvard UP, n.d.

Sample works-cited entries for books

17. Book by one author

The author's last name comes first, followed by a comma, the first name, and a period. For an edited book, follow the editor's name with a comma and the abbreviation *ed.*

Kavanagh, Peter, ed. Lapped Furrows. New York: Hand, 1969.

18. Two or more books by the same author

In the entry for the first book, include the author's name. In the second entry, substitute three hyphens and a period for the author's name. List the titles of books by the same author in alphabetical order.

Grimsley, Jim. Boulevard. Chapel Hill: Algonquin, 2002.

---. Dream Boy. New York: Simon, 1995.

19. Book by two or three authors

The second and subsequent authors' names appear first name first. A comma separates the authors' names. If all are editors, use *eds.* after the names.

Cruz, Arnaldo, and Martin Manalansan, eds. Queer Globalizations: Citizenship and the Afterlife of Colonialism. New York: New York UP, 2002.

20. Book by four or more authors

You may use the phrase *et al.* (meaning "and others") for all authors but the first, or you may write out all the names. You need to use the same method in the in-text citation as you do in the works-cited list.

Britton, Jane, et al., The Broadview Anthology of Expository Prose. New York: Broadview, 2001.

21. Book by an unknown author

Begin the entry with the title.

Encyclopedia of Americana. New York: Somerset, 2001.

22. Book by a group or organization

Treat the group as the author of the work.

United Nations. The Charter of the United Nations: A Commentary.
New York: Oxford UP, 2000.

23. Title within a title

If the title contains the title of another book or a word normally italicized, do not underline that title or word:

Higgins, Brian, and Hershel Parker. Critical Essays on Herman
Melville's Moby Dick. New York: Hall, 1992.

24. Book with no publication date

If no year of publication is given but can be approximated, put a *c.*
("circa") and the approximate date in brackets: [c. 1999]. Otherwise, put
n.d. ("no date").

O'Sullivan, Colin. Traditions and Novelties of the Irish Country Folk.
Dublin [c. 1793].

James, Franklin. In the Valley of the King. Cambridge: Harvard UP, n.d.

25. Reprinted works

For works of fiction that have been printed in many different editions
or reprints, give the original publication date after the title.

Wilde, Oscar. The Picture of Dorian Gray. 1890. New York: Norton,
2001.

26. Introduction, Foreword, Preface, or Afterword

Give the author and then the name of the specific part being cited. Next,
name the book. Then, if the author for the whole work is different, put that
author's name after the word *By.* Place inclusive page numbers at the end.

Benstock, Sheri. Introduction. The House of Mirth. By Edith Wharton.
Boston: Bedford-St. Martin's, 2002. 3-24.

27. Single chapter written by same author as the book

> Ardis, Ann. "Mapping the Middlebrow in Edwardian England."
> Modernism and Cultural Conflict: 1880-1922. Cambridge:
> Cambridge UP, 2002. 114-42.

28. Selection from an anthology or edited collection

> Sedaris, David. "Full House." The Best American Nonrequired
> Reading 2004. Ed. Dave Eggers. Boston: Houghton, 2004.
> 350-58.

29. More than one selection from an anthology or edited collection

Multiple selections from a single anthology can be handled by creating a complete entry for the anthology and shortened cross-references for individual works in that anthology.

> Adichie, Chimamanda Ngozi. "Half of a Yellow Sun." Eggers
> 1-17.

> Eggers, Dave, ed. The Best American Nonrequired Reading 2004.
> Boston: Houghton, 2004.

> Sedaris, David. "Full House." Eggers 350-58.

30. Article in a reference work

You can omit the names of editors and most publishing information for an article from a familiar reference work. Identify the edition by date. There is no need to give the page numbers when a work is arranged alphabetically. Give the author's name, if known.

> "Utilitarianism." The Columbia Encyclopedia. 6th ed.
> 2001.

31. Religious texts

> Holy Bible. King James Text: Modern Phrased Version. New York:
> Oxford UP, 1980.

32. Book with an editor

List an edited book under the editor's name if your focus is on the editor. Otherwise, cite an edited book under the author's name as shown in the second example.

Lewis, Gifford, ed. The Big House of Inver. By Edith Somerville and
    Martin Ross. Dublin: Farmar, 2000.

Somerville, Edith, and Martin Ross. The Big House of Inver. Ed.
    Gifford Lewis. Dublin: Farmar, 2000.

33. Book with a translator

Benjamin, Walter. The Arcades Project. Trans. Howard Eiland and
    Kevin McLaughlin. Cambridge: Harvard UP, 1999.

34. Second or subsequent edition of a book

Hawthorn, Jeremy, ed. A Concise Glossary of Contemporary Literary
    Theory. 3rd ed. London: Arnold, 2001.

35. Multivolume work

Identify both the volume you have used and the total number of volumes in the set.

Samuel, Raphael. Theatres of Memory. Vol. 1. London: Verso, 1999.
    2 vols.

If you refer to more than one volume, identify the specific volume in your in-text citations, and list the total number of volumes in Works Cited.

Samuel, Raphael. Theatres of Memory. 2 vols. London: Verso, 1999.

36. Book in a series

Give the series name just before the publishing information. Do not underline or italicize the series name.

Watson, James. William Faulkner: Self-Presentation and Performance.
    Literary Modernism Series. Austin: U of Texas P, 2000.

14d JOURNALS AND MAGAZINES IN MLA-STYLE WORKS CITED

JOURNAL COVER

CONTENTS PAGE

FIRST PAGE OF ARTICLE

Author's name

Title of article

Abstract of article

Name of journal, volume number, issue number, date of publication, page number

Selber, Stuart A. "Reimagining the Functional Side of Computer Literacy." CCC 55 (2004): 470-503.

AUTHOR'S NAME

The author's last name comes first, followed by a comma and the first name.

For two or more works by the same author, consult the sample list of Works Cited on page 99–100.

TITLE OF ARTICLE

Use the exact title, which appears at the top of the article.

Put the title in quotation marks. If a book title is part of the article's title, underline the book title. If a title requiring quotation marks is part of the article's title, use single quotation marks.

All nouns, verbs, pronouns, adjectives, adverbs, and subordinating conjunctions, and the first word of the title are capitalized. Do not capitalize any article, preposition, coordinating conjunction, or *to* in an infinitive, unless it is the first word of the title.

PUBLICATION INFORMATION

Name of journal

Underline the title of the journal.

Abbreviate the title of the journal if it commonly appears that way (as in this example).

Volume, issue, and page numbers

- For journals paginated separately by issue, list the volume number, a period, and then the issue number before the year and page numbers.
- For continuously paginated journals, include the volume number before the year, but do *not* include the issue number.

Date of publication

- For magazines and journals identified by the month or season of publication, use the month (or season) and year in place of the volume number.
- For weekly or biweekly magazines, give both the day and month of publication, as listed on the issue. Note that the day precedes the month and no comma is used.

Sample works-cited entries for journals and magazines

37. Article by one author

Mallory, Anne. "Burke, Boredom, and the Theater of
Counterrevolution." PMLA 119 (2003): 329-43.

38. Article by two or three authors

Shamoo, Adil E., and Jonathan D. Moreo. "Ethics of Research
Involving Mandatory Drug Testing of High School Athletes." The
American Journal of Bioethics 1 (2004): 25-31.

39. Article by four or more authors

You may use the phrase *et al.* (meaning "and others") for all authors
but the first, or you may write out all the names.

Breece, Katherine E., et al. "Patterns of mtDNA Diversity in
Northwestern North America." Human Biology 76 (2004): 33-54.

40. Article by an unknown author

"Idol Gossip." People Magazine 12 Apr. 2004: 34-35.

41. Monthly or seasonal magazines or journals

Use the month (or season) and year in place of the volume number.
Abbreviate the names of all months except May, June, and July.

Barlow, John Perry. "Africa Rising: Everything You Know about Africa
Is Wrong." Wired Jan. 1998: 142-58.

42. Weekly or biweekly magazines

Give both the day and month of publication, as listed on the issue.

Toobin, Jeffrey. "Crackdown." New Yorker 5 Nov. 2001: 56-61.

43. Article in a journal paginated by volume

Include the volume number before the year and page numbers, but do not include the issue number.

Lerer, Seth. "Medieval English Literature and the Idea of the
Anthology." PMLA 118 (2003): 1251-67.

44. Article in a journal paginated by issue

List the volume number, a period, and then the issue number (here, *2/3*) before the year and page numbers.

Davis, Jim. "Rethinking Globalization." Race and Class 40.2/3 (1999):
37-48.

45. Review

If there is no title, just name the work reviewed.

Mendelsohn, Daniel. "The Two Oscar Wildes." Rev. of The Importance
of Being Earnest, dir. Oliver Parker. New York Review of Books
10 Oct. 2002: 23-24.

46. Letter to the editor

Patai, Daphne. Letter. Harper's Magazine Dec. 2001: 4.

47. Editorial

"Stop Stonewalling on Reform." Editorial. Business Week 17 June
2002: 108.

14e NEWSPAPERS IN MLA-STYLE WORKS CITED

Date of publication

Name of newspaper

MASTHEAD OF THE NEWSPAPER AS IT APPEARS ON THE FRONT PAGE

Title of article

FIRST PAGE OF ARTICLE (PAGE B1)

Author's name

CONTINUATION OF ARTICLE (PAGE B5)

Anderson, Curt. "Feds Reopen Emmett Till Murder Investigation."

Daily Camera [Boulder] 11 May 2004: B1+.

AUTHOR'S NAME

The author's last name comes first, followed by a comma and the first name.

For two or more works by the same author, consult the sample Works Cited list on page 100.

TITLE OF ARTICLE

Use the exact title, which appears at the top of the article.

Put the title in quotation marks. If a book title is part of the article's title, underline the book title. If a title requiring quotation marks is part of the article's title, use single quotation marks.

All nouns, verbs, pronouns, adjectives, adverbs, subordinating conjunctions, and the first word of the title are capitalized. Do not capitalize any article, preposition, coordinating conjunction, or *to* in an infinitive, unless it is the first word of the title.

PUBLICATION INFORMATION

Name of newspaper

Underline the name.

Omit introductory articles (New York Times, *not* The New York Times).

If the city is not mentioned in the name of the paper, add it in square brackets after the name of the newspaper.

Date of publication and edition

Give the complete date for a newspaper—day, month, and year.

Abbreviate the names of all months except May, June, and July.

Do *not* give the volume and issue numbers for a newspaper.

Specify the edition if one is given on the masthead: *natl. ed., final ed., suburban ed.*

Place a colon after the edition if an edition name or number is given. If no edition is listed, place the colon after the date.

Section and page numbers

Provide the section label (usually A, B, C, etc.).

Include the page number. If the article continues to a nonconsecutive page, add a plus sign after the number of the first page.

Sample works-cited entries for newspapers

48. Article by one author

Boyd, Robert S. "Solar System Has a Double." Montreal Gazette 14
June 2002, final ed.: A1.

49. Article by two or three authors

Davis, Howard, June Allstead, and Jane Mavis. "Rice's Testimony to
9/11 Commission Leaves Unanswered Questions." Dallas
Morning News 9 Apr. 2004, final ed.: C5.

50. Article by an unknown author

"Democratic Candidates Debate Iraq War." Austin American-Statesman
19 Jan. 2004: A6.

51. Article that continues to a nonconsecutive page

Add a plus sign after the number of the first page.

Kaplow, Larry, and Tasgola Karla Bruner. "U.S.: Don't Let Taliban Forces
Flee." Austin American-Statesman 20 Nov. 2001, final ed.: A1+.

52. Review

Fox, Nichols. "What's for Dinner?" Rev. of Eating in the Dark:
America's Experiment with Genetically Engineered Food, by
Kathleen Hart. Washington Post 16 June 2002: T9.

53. Letter to the editor

Canavan, Jim. Letter. Boston Globe Dec. 2001: 4.

54. Editorial

Dowd, Maureen. "The Iraqi Inversion." Editorial. New York Times 8
Apr. 2004, late ed.: A11.

If the editorial is unsigned, put the title first.

14f GOVERNMENT DOCUMENTS, PAMPHLETS, DISSERTATIONS, AND LETTERS IN MLA-STYLE WORKS CITED

55. Government documents

United States. Office of the Surgeon General. The Health
    Consequences of Involuntary Smoking: A Report of the Surgeon
    General. Rockville: U.S. Public Health Service, 1986.

56. *Congressional Record*

Cong. Rec. 8 Feb. 2000: 1222-46.

57. Bulletin or pamphlet

If there is no author, try to mention the document in the text.

The Common Cold. Austin: U of Texas Health Center, 2001.

58. Published letter

Wilde, Oscar. "To Lord Alfred Douglas." 17 Feb. 1895. In The Complete
    Letters of Oscar Wilde. Ed. Merlin Holland and Rupert Hart-
    Davis. New York: Holt, 2000. 632-33.

59. Unpublished letter

Mentioning the letter and the information from the letter in the text
itself is preferable to a parenthetical citation.

Welty, Eudora. Letter to Elizabeth Bowen. 1 May 1951. Harry Ransom
    Humanities Research Center, Austin.

60. Published dissertation or thesis

Mason, Jennifer. Civilized Creatures: Animality, Cultural Power, and
    American Literature, 1850–1901. Diss. U of Texas at Austin,
    2000. Ann Arbor: UMI, 2000. 9992865.

14g   ONLINE PUBLICATIONS IN MLA-STYLE WORKS CITED

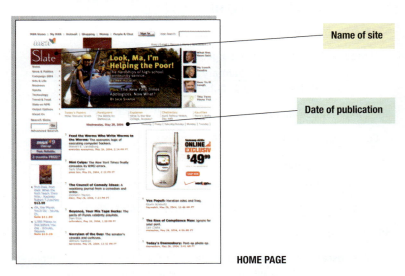

Name of site

Date of publication

HOME PAGE

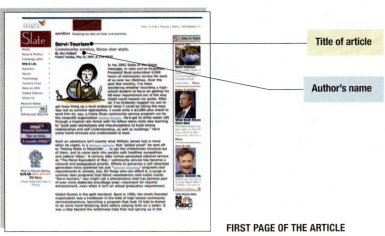

Title of article

Author's name

FIRST PAGE OF THE ARTICLE

> Hulbert, Ann. "Servi-Tourism: Community Service, Three-Star Style."
>
> Slate 26 May 2004. 30 May 2004 <http://slate.msn.com/id/210125/>.

AUTHOR'S NAME

Authorship is sometimes hard to discern for online sources. If you know the author or creator, follow the rules for books and journals.

If the only authority you find is a group or organization, list its name after the date of publication or last revision.

TITLE OF PAGE OR ARTICLE AND NAME OF SITE

- The name of a Web site will usually be found on its index or home page. If you cannot find a link back to the home page on the page you are on, look at the URL for clues. You can work your way back through the URL, deleting sections (separated by slashes) until you come to a home or index page.

- If there is no title for the Web site, list it by author or creator. If it is a personal home page, place the words *Home page* after the name of the owner of the page.

PUBLICATION INFORMATION

Dates

List two dates for each Web site.

1. List the date the site was produced or last revised (often at the bottom of the page; might also be a copyright date) after the name of the site. This date might be just a year.
2. List the date you accessed the site. Place this second date just before the URL. Notice that there is no period after the date of access.

URLs

Copy the address exactly as it appears in your browser window. You can even copy and paste the address into your text for greater accuracy. Put it in angle brackets followed by a period.

Common Questions about Citing Online Sources

Where do I find the title?

Web sites are often made up of many separate pages or articles. Each page or article on a Web site may or may not have a title. If you are citing a page that has a title, treat the title like that of an article in a periodical. Otherwise, treat the name of the Web site itself as you would a book.

How do I handle very long URLs?

If the URL is excessively long and complicated, give the URL of the site's search page. If the document is from a subscription service, give the URL of the service's home page or the keyword assigned, preceded by the word *Keyword.* You can also give the sequence of links you followed, preceded by the word *Path.* Place a colon after *Keyword* or *Path.*

Note: Be sure to test your URLs as part of your proofreading process.

Sample works-cited entries for online publications

61. Publication by a known author

Follow the rules for periodicals and books.

Boerner, Steve. "Leopold Mozart." The Mozart Project: Biography. Ed. Steve Boerner. 21 Mar. 1998. The Mozart Project. 30 Dec. 2004 <http://www.mozartproject.org/biography/mozart_l.html>.

62. Publication by a group or organization

If the only authority you find is a group or organization, list its name after the date of publication or date of revision.

"State of the Birds, USA 2004." Audubon. 2004. National Audubon Society. 19 Nov. 2004 <http://www.audubon.org/bird/stateofthebirds/>.

63. Publication with an author and a group affiliation

List the name of the organization or institution after the publication date or revision date.

> Edwards, Rebecca. "Socialism." 1896. 2000. Vassar College.
>   20 Nov. 2001 <http://iberia.vassar.edu/1896/
>   socialism.html#debs>.

64. Publication where the author's name is a pseudonym

> Akma. "Still Recouping." Akma's Random Thoughts. Weblog posting.
>   16 Feb. 2005. 21 Feb. 2005 <http://akma.disseminary.org>.

65. Article in a scholarly journal

The volume and issue number follow the name of the journal. The date in parentheses is the date of publication.

> Caramanica, Laura. "Shared Governance: Hartford Hospital's
>   Experience." Online Journal of Issues in Nursing 9.1 (Jan.
>   2004). 12 Apr. 2004 <http://www.nursingworld.org/ojin/
>   topic23/tpc23_2.htm/>.

66. Article in a newspaper

The first date is the date of publication, the second is the date of access.

> Erard, Michael. "A Colossal Wreck." Austin Chronicle 16 Nov. 2001. 21
>   Nov. 2001 <http://www.austinchronicle.com/issues/
>   dispatch/2001-11-16/pols_feature.html>.

67. Article in a popular magazine

The first date is the date of publication, the second is the date of access.

> Cohen, Jesse. "When Harry Met Maggie." Slate 16 Nov. 2001. 21 Nov.
>   2001 <http://slate.msn.com/?id=2058733&>.

68. Online book

Prebish, Charles S., and Kenneth K. Tanaka. The Faces of Buddhism in
America. Berkeley: U of California P, 2003. 22 May 2004
<http://ark.cdlib.org/ark:/13030/ft1v19n7k4/>.

69. Online scholarly project or database

If you are citing a page that has a title, treat the title like that of an article in a periodical. Otherwise, treat the name of the Web site itself as you would a book, as in the following example.

The Valley of the Shadow: Two Communities in the American
Civil War. Ed. Edward L. Ayres, 2001. Virginia Center for
Digital History, U of Virginia. 1 July 2002 <http://
www.iath.virginia.edu/vshadow2/>.

70. Document within a scholarly project or database

Give the author and title of the work first, as well as its date and place of publication if it is a book. Then give the name of the project or database, its editor, version or revision date, affiliation, and date of access. The address is the address of the document itself.

Calhoun, John C. "The Southern Address." Nineteenth Century
Documents Project. Ed. Lloyd Bensen. 2000. Furman U.
21 Nov. 2001 <http://www.furman.edu/~benson/docs/
calhoun.htm>.

71. Work from a library database (see Source Sample on p. 47)

Begin with the print publication information, then the name of the database (underlined), the name of the vendor, the name of the library or library system, date of access, and the URL of the vendor's home page.

Snider, Michael. "Wired to Another World." Maclean's 3 March 2003:
23-24. Academic Search Premier. EBSCO. Harold B. Lee Lib.,
Brigham Young U. 14 March 2003 <http://www.epnet.com/>.

72. Work from a personal subscription service

"Anasazi." Compton's Encyclopedia Online. Vers. 2.0. 1997. America
  Online. 12 Dec. 2001. Keyword: Compton's.

73. Online government publication

United States. Dept. of the Treasury. Everyday Tax Solutions. Mar.
  2004. 12 Apr. 2004 <http://www.irs.gov/individuals/article/
  0,,id=119857,00.html>.

14h CD-ROM, SOFTWARE, AND UNEDITED ONLINE SOURCES IN MLA-STYLE WORKS CITED

74. CD-ROM by a known author

Hagen, Edward, and Phillip Walker. Human Evolution: A Multimedia Guide
  to the Fossil Record. 2002 ed. CD-ROM. New York: Norton, 2002.

75. Periodically revised database on CD-ROM

Provide the publication dates for the article you are citing as well as for the data disc itself.

Roper, Jill. "Why Don't We Teach Reading in High School?" Journal of
  Secondary Education 22 (1999): 423-40. ProQuest General
  Periodicals. CD-ROM. UMI-ProQuest. June 2000.

76. Computer software

Provide the author's name (if known), the version number (if any), the manufacturer, and the date. For in-text notes, mentioning the software in the text itself is preferable to a parenthetical citation.

AOL. Vers. 9.0. America Online, 2004.

77. Email communication

Wilson, Samuel. Email to the author. 18 Sept. 2002.

78. Course home page

Kirkpatrick, Judith. American Literature Online. Course home page.
Jan.-May 2003. Dept. of English. Kapi'olani CC. 21 Feb. 2003.
<http://www2.hawaii.edu/~kirkpatr/s03/s03250syllabus.html>.

79. Personal home page

If there is no title for the Web site, list it by author or creator. Place the
words *Home page* after the name of the owner of the page.

Stallman, Richard. Home page. 21 Mar. 2004. 8 Apr. 2004
<http://www.stallman.org/>.

14i VISUAL SOURCES IN MLA-STYLE WORKS CITED

80. Cartoon

Chast, Roz. "Are You in Your Goddess Years?" Cartoon. New Yorker 10
Mar. 2004: 113.

81. Advertisement

Discover Card. Advertisement. Newsweek 29 Oct. 2001: 40-41.

82. Map, graph, or chart

Baltimore Street Map and Visitor's Guide. Map. Baltimore: MAP, 1999.

83. Painting, sculpture, or photograph

Provide the artist's name, the title of the work, the name of the institution or individual who owns the work, and the city. If you are citing a photograph of a work, give the information for the work, followed by the publication information for the source that you got the photograph from. Include
the slide, plate, figure, or page number, as relevant. In the text, mentioning
the work and the artist in the text itself is preferable to a parenthetical citation.

Cloar, Carroll. Odie Maude. 1990. David Lusk Gallery, Memphis.

14j MULTIMEDIA SOURCES IN MLA-STYLE WORKS CITED

84. Sound recording

Williams, Lucinda. Essence. Lost Highway Records, 2001.

85. Film

Lost in Translation. Dir. Sofia Coppola. Perf. Bill Murray and Scarlett Johansson. Focus Features, 2003.

86. Video or DVD

List the medium (DVD, VHS) before the name of the distributor.

House of Flying Daggers. Dir. Yimou Zhang. Perf. Takeshi Kaneshiro and Ziyi Zhang. DVD. Columbia Tristar, 2005.

87. Television or radio program

Provide the title of the episode or segment, followed by the title of the program and series (if any). After the titles, list any performers, narrators, directors, or others who might be pertinent. Then give the name of the network, call numbers and city for any local station, and the broadcast date.

"The Gift." Buffy the Vampire Slayer. Perf. Sarah Michelle Gellar and Alyson Hannigan. Fox. 22 May 2001.

88. Interview

Give the name of the person you interviewed first, then the kind of interview (personal, telephone, or email) and the date the interview took place.

Williams, Robin. Personal interview. 15 May 2004.

89. Speech, debate, mediated discussion, or public talk

Clinton, William Jefferson. Liz Carpenter Distinguished Lecture Series, U of Texas at Austin. 12 Feb. 2003.

14k SAMPLE RESEARCH PAPER AND WORKS-CITED PAGES

Walker 1

Ashley Walker

Professor Avalos

English 102

2 December 2003

Include your last name and page number as page header, beginning with the first page, 1/2" from the top.

MLA style does not require a title page. Check with your instructor to find out whether you need one.

Center the title. Do not underline the title, put it inside quotation marks, or type it in all capital letters.

Specify 1" margins all around. Double-space everything.

Preventing Obesity in Children

Americans are the fattest people on the planet and continue to expand. According to a survey of adult men and women in the United States during 1999-2000, published in JAMA: The Journal of the American Medical Association, 30.5% of Americans are obese, up from 22.9% ten years earlier, and nearly two-thirds (64.5%) are overweight (Flegal et al. 1723). Excess weight isn't just a matter of looks. Obesity magnifies the risk of heart disease, diabetes, high blood pressure, and other ailments—already overtaking tobacco as the leading cause of chronic illness (Brownell and Horgen 4). An especially disturbing aspect of this trend is that children are increasingly obese. The Centers for Disease Control and Prevention reports that the percentage of obese children aged 6 to 11 almost quadrupled from 4% in 1974 to 15% in 2000, and the percentage of obese children aged 12 to 19 increased from

Walker 2

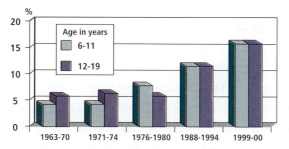

NOTES: Excludes pregnant women starting with 1971-74. Pregnancy status not available for 1963-65 and 1966-70. Data for 1963-65 are for children 6-11 years of age, data for 1966-70 are for adolescents 12-17 years of age, not 12-19 years.
SOURCE CDC/NCHS, NHES and NHANES.

Fig. 1. Prevalence of overweight among children and adolescents ages 6-19 years, chart from United States, Department of Health and Human Services, Centers for Disease Control and Prevention, Prevalence of Overweight among Children and Adolescents: United States, 1999-2000 (24 Oct. 2002 <http://www.cdc.gov/nchs/products/pubs/pubd/ hestats/overwght99.htm>).

6% in 1974 to 15% in 2000 (United States; see Fig. 1). Obese children have a 70% chance of becoming obese adults with a much higher risk of serious illness than those of normal weight (Brownell and Horgen 46). Furthermore, obese children suffer many serious health problems today. Pediatricians now routinely treat atherosclerosis and type II

Walker 3

diabetes, diseases that used to be frequent only among older people (Tyre 38). Today's children are among the first generation in American history who may die at earlier ages than their parents.

For most people in the United States, obesity is a matter of individual choice and old-fashioned willpower (Lee and Oliver). The usual advice for overweight people is to eat less and exercise more, but how applicable is this advice for children unless they have strong guidance from adults? How can children make intelligent choices about eating in an environment where overeating is normal and where few adults know what's in the food they eat? The United States has been successful in addressing teenage health problems: drug use has dropped, teenage pregnancy has been reduced, and teen smoking has declined. We need to take a similar proactive response by taking concrete steps to reverse the trend toward more obese children.

Many have blamed the rise in obesity on a more sedentary life style, including the move to the suburbs, where people drive instead of walk, and increased viewing of television. One study of children watching television found a significant drop in the average metabolic rate during viewing (Klesges, Shelton, and Klesges).

Indent each paragraph five spaces (1/2" on the ruler in your word processing program).

Walker's thesis appears here, at the end of her second paragraph. The preceding questions establish a context for her thesis.

Walker 4

Another study reports that viewing also affects their eating behavior (Robinson and Killen). No doubt that children who exercise less tend to weigh more, but the couch potato argument does not explain why the enormous weight gains have occurred over the past twenty-five years. The move to the suburbs and the widespread viewing of television began in the 1950s. Furthermore, the couch potato argument neglects the extraordinary rise of female participation in athletics. The number of young women playing a sport in high school has risen from 294,015 in 1971-72 to 2,856,358 in 2002-03, almost a tenfold increase ("Participation"). Yet girls, like boys, have gained weight.

The patterns of eating in America have changed over the past three decades. With more people working longer hours and fewer staying at home, annual spending in adjusted dollars at restaurants increased nearly by a factor of ten between 1970 and 2003, from $42.8 billion to $426.1 billion ("Industry"). The growth was most rapid among fast-food chains, which by 1999 were opening a new restaurant every two hours (Schlosser, "Bitter").

Cite publications by the name of the author (or authors).

Sources not identified with an author are referenced in text by title.

Do not include a page number for items without pagination, such as Web sites.

Walker 5

If more than one publication is by the same author, include an abbreviated title in the reference.

Quotations of more than four lines should be indented 1" or ten spaces. Do not use quotation marks. Introduce block quotations rather than just dropping them into the text.

According to Eric Schlosser,

> In 1970, Americans spent about $6 billion on fast food; in 2001, they spent more than $110 billion. Americans now spend more money on fast food than on higher education, personal computers, computer software, or new cars. They spend more money on fast food than on movies, books, magazines, newspapers, videos, and recorded music—combined. (Fast 3)

As the restaurant business became more competitive, fast-food chains realized that the cost of the food they served was small in comparison to the costs of buildings, labor, packaging, and advertising, so they began increasing the size of portions. Amanda Spake and Mary Brophy Marcus note: "When McDonald's opened, its original burger, fries, and 12-ounce Coke provided 590 calories. Today, a supersize Extra Value Meal with a Quarter Pounder With Cheese, supersize fries, and a supersize drink is 1,550 calories" (44). Large portions may represent good value for the dollar, but they are not good value for overall health.

Works Cited

Barboza, David. "If You Pitch It, They Will Eat." New York

Times 3 Aug. 2003, late ed., sec. C: 1+.

Brownell, Kelly D. "Get Slim with Higher Taxes." New York

Times 15 Dec. 1994, late ed.: A29.

Brownell, Kelly D., and Katherine Battle Horgen. Food

Fight: The Inside Story of the Food Industry,

America's Obesity Crisis, and What We Can Do

about It. Chicago: Contemporary, 2004.

"CCF Ad Campaigns." ConsumerFreedom.com. 2003.

Center for Consumer Freedom. 18 Nov. 2003 <http://

www.consumerfreedom.com/ad_campaign.cfm>.

Flegal, Katherine M., et al. "Prevalence and Trends in

Obesity among US Adults, 1999-2000." JAMA 188

(2002): 1723-27.

"Participation Summary 2002-03." Make a Difference. 2003.

National Federation of State High School Associations.

14 Nov. 2003 <http://www.nfhs.org/

nf_survey_resources.asp>.

Robinson, Thomas N., and Joel D. Killen. "Obesity

Prevention for Children and Adolescents." Body Image,

Eating Disorders, and Obesity in Youth: Assessment,

Prevention, and Treatment. Ed. J. Kevin Thompson and

Linda Smolak. Washington: APA, 2001. 261-92.

Center "Works Cited" on a new page.

Double-space all entries. Indent all but the first line in each entry five spaces.

Alphabetize entries by the last names of the authors or by the first important word in the title if no author is listed.

Underline the titles of books and periodicals.

Walker 7

Schlosser, Eric. "The Bitter Truth about Fast Food."

Guardian 7 Apr. 2001, weekend sec.: 13.

---. Fast Food Nation: The Dark Side of the All-American

Meal. New York: Perennial, 2002.

Spake, Amanda, and Mary Brophy Marcus. "A Fat Nation."

U.S. News & World Report 19 Aug. 2002: 40-47.

Tyre, Peg. "Fighting 'Big Fat.'" Newsweek 5 Aug. 2002:

38-40.

Uhlenhuth, Karen. "Spoonful of Sugar Makes Appetites

Go Up." Advertiser 19 Jan. 2003: 39. LexisNexis

Academic. LexisNexis. Perry-Casteñeda Lib., U of

Texas at Austin. 20 Nov. 2003 <http://

www.lexis-nexis.com/>.

United States. Department of Health and Human Services.

Centers for Disease Control and Prevention.

Prevalence of Overweight among Children and

Adolescents: United States, 1999-2000. 24 Oct. 2002.

10 Nov. 2003 <http://www.cdc.gov/nchs/products/

pubs/pubd/ hestats/overwght99.htm>.

Walker, Andrea K. "Chipping Away at Fat." Baltimore Sun

26 Sept. 2003, final ed.: C1. LexisNexis Academic.

LexisNexis. Perry-Casteñeda Lib., U of Texas at

Austin. 20 Nov. 2003 <http://www.lexis-nexis.com/>.

If an author has more than one entry, list the entries in alphabetical order by title. Use three hyphens in place of the author's name for the second and subsequent entries.

Go through your text and make sure all the sources you have used are in the list of works cited.

CHAPTER 15

APA Documentation

Social sciences disciplines, including government, linguistics, psychology, sociology, and education, frequently use the American Psychological Association (APA) documentation style. For a detailed treatment of APA style, consult the *Publication Manual of the American Psychological Association*, fifth edition (2001).

15a THE ELEMENTS OF APA DOCUMENTATION

APA style emphasizes the date of publication. When you cite an author's name in the body of your paper, always include the date of publication. Notice too that APA style includes the abbreviation for page (p.) in front of the page number. A comma separates each element of the citation.

> Zukin (2004) observes that teens today begin to shop for themselves at age 13 or 14, "the same age when lower-class children, in the past, became apprentices or went to work in factories" (p. 50).

If the author's name is not mentioned in the sentence, the reference looks like this:

> One sociologist notes that teens today begin to shop for themselves at age 13 or 14, "the same age when lower-class children, in the past, became apprentices or went to work in factories" (Zukin, 2004, p. 50).

The corresponding entry in the references list would be

> Zukin, S. (2004). *Point of purchase: How shopping changed American culture*. New York: Routledge.

See Section 15g, page 119, for a sample reference list.

15b SAMPLE IN-TEXT CITATIONS IN APA STYLE

When Do You Need to Give a Page Number?

- Give the page number for all direct quotations.
- For electronic sources that do not provide page numbers, give the paragraph number when available. Use the abbreviation *para.* or the symbol ¶.
- If the source does not include page numbers, it is preferable to reference the work and the author in the text.

  In Wes Anderson's 1998 film *Rushmore,* . . .

- You do *not* need to provide page numbers when paraphrasing or referring to ideas in other works.

1. Author named in your text

Influential sociologist Daniel Bell (1973) noted a shift in the United States to the "postindustrial society" (p. 3).

2. Author not named in your text

In 1997, the Gallup poll reported that 55% of adults in the United States think secondhand smoke is "very harmful," compared to only 36% in 1994 (Saad, 1997, p. 4).

3. Work by a single author

(Bell, 1973, p. 3)

4. Work by two authors

(Suzuki & Irabu, 2002, p. 404)

5. Work by three to five authors

The authors' last names follow the order of the title page:

(Francisco, Vaughn, & Romano, 2001, p. 7)

Subsequent references can use the first name and *et al.*

(Francisco et al., 2001, p. 17)

6. Work by six or more authors

Use the first author's last name and *et al.* for all in-text references:

(Swallit et al., 2004, p. 49)

7. Work by a group or organization

Identify the group author in the text and place only the page number in the parentheses:

The National Organization for Women (2001) observed that this "generational shift in attitudes towards marriage and childrearing" will have profound consequences (p. 325).

8. Work by an unknown author

Use a shortened version of the title (or the full title if it is short) in place of the author's name. Capitalize all key words in the title. If it is an article title, place it in quotation marks.

("Derailing the Peace Process," 2003, p. 44)

9. Two works by one author with the same copyright date

Assign the dates letters (a, b, etc.) according to their alphabetical arrangement in the references list.

The majority of books written about coauthorship focus on partners of the same sex (Laird, 2001a, p. 351).

10. Two or more sources within the same sentence
Place each citation directly after the statement it supports.

Some surveys report an increase in homelessness rates (Alford, 2004) while others chart a slight decrease (Rice, 2003a) . . .

If you need to cite two or more works within the same parentheses, list them in the order they appear in the references list and separate them with a semicolon.

(Alford, 2004; Rice, 2003a)

11. Work quoted in another source
Name the work and give a citation for the secondary source.

Saunders and Kellman's study (as cited in McAtee, Luhan, Stiles, & Buell, 1994)

12. Quotations 40 words or longer
Indent long quotations five spaces and omit quotation marks. Note that the period appears before the parentheses in an indented "block" quote.

Orlean (2001) has attempted to explain the popularity of the painter Thomas Kinkade:

People like to own things they think are valuable. . . . The high price of limited editions is part of their appeal; it implies that they are choice and exclusive, and that only a certain class of people will be able to afford them. (p. 128)

15c BOOKS AND NONPERIODICAL SOURCES IN THE APA-STYLE REFERENCES LIST

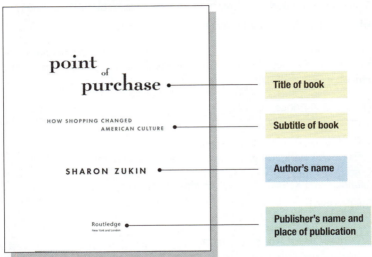

point of purchase • Title of book

HOW SHOPPING CHANGED AMERICAN CULTURE • Subtitle of book

SHARON ZUKIN • Author's name

Routledge
New York and London • Publisher's name and place of publication

TITLE PAGE

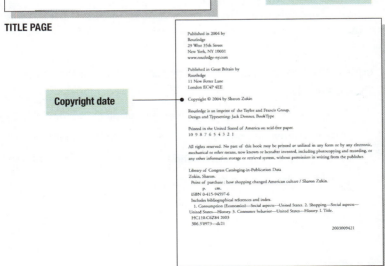

Published in 2004 by
Routledge
29 West 35th Street
New York, NY 10001
www.routledge-ny.com

Published in Great Britain by
Routledge
11 New Fetter Lane
London EC4P 4EE

Copyright © 2004 by Sharon Zukin — **Copyright date**

Routledge is an imprint of the Taylor and Francis Group.
Design and Typesetting: Jack Donner, BookType

Printed in the United Stated of America on acid-free paper.
10 9 8 7 6 5 4 3 2 1

All rights reserved. No part of this book may be printed or utilized in any form or by any electronic, mechanical or other means, now known or hereafter invented, including photocopying and recording, or any other information storage or retrieval system, without permission in writing from the publisher.

Library of Congress Cataloging-in-Publication Data
Zukin, Sharon.
    Point of purchase : how shopping changed American culture / Sharon Zukin.
        p.   cm.
    ISBN 0-415-94597-6
    Includes bibliographical references and index.
        1. Consumption (Economics)—Social aspects—United States. 2. Shopping—Social aspects—United States—History. 3. Consumer behavior—United States—History. I. Title.
    HC110.C6Z84 2003
    306.3'0973—dc21
                                                        2003009421

COPYRIGHT PAGE

Zukin, S. (2004). *Point of purchase: How shopping changed American culture*. New York: Routledge.

AUTHOR'S OR EDITOR'S NAME

The author's last name comes first, followed by a comma and the author's initials.

If an editor, put the abbreviation *Ed.* in parentheses after the name.

Kavanagh, P. (Ed.).

BOOK TITLE

- Italicize the title (or underline, if you are working on a typewriter).
- Capitalize only the first word, proper nouns, and the first word after a colon.
- If the title is in a foreign language, copy it exactly as it appears on the title page.

YEAR OF PUBLICATION

- Give the year the work was copyrighted in parentheses.
- If no year of publication is given, write *n.d.* ("no date") in parentheses:

Smith, S. (n.d.).

- If it is a multivolume edited work, published over a period of more than one year, put the span in parentheses:

Smith, S. (1999–2001).

PUBLICATION INFORMATION

Place of publication

- List the city without a state abbreviation or country for major cities known for publishing (New York, Boston).
- Add the state abbreviation or country for other cities (Foster City, CA). If the publisher is a university named for a state, omit the state abbreviation.
- If more than one city is given on the title page, list only the first.

Publisher's name

Do not shorten or abbreviate words like *University* or *Press*. Omit words such as *Co.*, *Inc.*, and *Publishers*.

Sample references for books

13. Book by one author

Ball, E. (2000). *Slaves in the family*. New York: Ballantine Books.

For edited works, use the abbreviation *Ed.* in parentheses.

Kavanagh, P. (Ed.). (1969). *Lapped furrows*. New York: Hand Press.

14. Two or more books by the same author
Arrange according to the date, with the earlist publication first.

Jules, R. (2003). *Internal memos and other classified documents*. London: Hutchinson.
Jules, R. (2004). *Derelict cabinet*. London: Corgi-Transworld.

15. Book by two authors

Hardt, M., & Negri, A. (2000). *Empire*. Cambridge, MA: Harvard University Press.

For edited works, use *(Eds.)* after the names.

McClelland, D., & Eismann, K. (Eds.).

16. Book by three or more authors
The seventh and subsequent authors can be abbreviated to *et al.*

Anders, K., Child, H., Davis, K., Logan, O., Petersen, J., Tymes, J., et al.

17. Book by an unknown author

Survey of Developing Nations. (2003). New York: Justice for All Press.

18. Book by a group or organization

Centers for Disease Control and Prevention. (2003). *Men and heart disease: An atlas of racial and ethnic disparities in mortality.* Atlanta, GA: Author.

19. Chapter in an edited collection

Howard, A. (1997). Labor, history, and sweatshops in the new global economy. In A. Ross (Ed.), *No sweat: Fashion, free trade, and the rights of garment workers* (pp. 151–172). New York: Verso.

20. Article in a reference work

Viscosity. (2001). *The Columbia encyclopedia* (6th ed.). New York: Columbia University Press.

21. Government document

When the author and publisher are identical, use the word *Author* as the name of the publisher.

U.S. Environmental Protection Agency. (2002). *Respiratory health effects of passive smoking: Lung cancer and other disorders.* (EPA Publication No. 600/6-90/006 F). Washington, DC: Author.

22. Religious or classical texts

Reference entries are not required for major classical works or the Bible, but in the first in-text citation, identify the edition used.

John 3.16 (Modern Phrased Version)

15d PERIODICAL SOURCES IN THE APA-STYLE REFERENCES LIST

COMMUNICATION EDUCATION

(ISSN 0363-4523) VOLUME 52 • NUMBER 1 • JANUARY 2003

Name of journal, volume, issue number, date

ARTICLES

In the last decade engineering education and industry have requested assistance from communication educators. Responding to increased attention on the changing expectations for practicing engineers and an attendant need for better communication skills, these teams of engineering and communication educators have been working to incorporate speaking and writing in engineering education. Despite a great deal of anecdotal evidence that communication is important to working engineers, relatively little data based information is available to help us understand better the specifics of how and why communication is important for these particular professionals. This paper reports the results of practicing engineers' descriptions of the importance of oral communication. These data suggest that engineering practice takes place in an intensely oral culture and while formal presentations are important to practicing engineers, daily work is characterized more by interpersonal and small group experiences. Communication skills such as translation, clarity, negotiation, and listening are vital.

This study explored the relationship between academic mentoring behaviors and the organizational socialization of new faculty members within the communication discipline. Participants included 259 faculty members from the National Communication Association. Results indicated that mentors' tendencies to provide support and encouragement, a sense of collegiality, and research assistance are related to an organizational newcomer's feelings of connectedness and ownership with the work environment. Overall, the results suggested that the benefits of mentoring are reciprocal and benefit the institution as well as the protégé.

Amidst few empirical studies of the effects of high stakes testing on classroom talk, this study concretely illustrates erosion of inclusive teacher-student interaction. Using discourse analysis, it compares K-12 classroom instructional practices before and after the imposition of standardized testing practices. Before testing mandates: 1) diversity was regarded as a resource for opportunities to learn something valuable; 2) standards for academic achievement provided a wide range of possible performances; 3) teachers and students were flexible in their stances toward what constituted academic performance; 4) students' constructed student "selves" were part of a dialogue about academic expectations; and 5) students' personal texts were a legitimate part of the curriculum. In test-impacted classrooms, in contrast,

CONTENTS PAGE

Practicing Engineers Talk about the Importance of Talk: A Report on the Role of Oral Communication in the Workplace

Ann L. Darling and Deanna P. Dannels

Title of article

Authors' names

Abstract

In the last decade engineering education and industry have requested assistance from communication educators. Responding to increased attention on the changing expectations for practicing engineers and an attendant need for better communication skills, these teams of engineering and communication educators have been working to incorporate speaking and writing in engineering education. Despite a great deal of anecdotal evidence that communication is important to working engineers, relatively little data based information is available to help us understand better the specifics of how and why communication is important for these particular professionals. This paper reports the results of practicing engineers' descriptions of the importance of oral communication. These data suggest that engineering practice takes place in an intensely oral culture and while formal presentations are important to practicing engineers, daily work is characterized more by interpersonal and small group experiences. Communication skills such as translation, clarity, negotiation, and listening are vital. **Keywords:** communication in the professions, workplace teams, engineering education, oral presentations

Increasingly, oral communication is recognized as an essential element of the curriculum in technical disciplines (Beaufait, 1991; Bjorklund & Colbeck, 2001; Denton, 1998; Yu & Liaw, 1998). Disciplines such as biology, chemistry, engineering, and mathematics, with a long curricular tradition focused on technical knowledge, have begun to explore the role of oral performance as both a learning tool (e.g., use of cooperative learning groups) and outcome (i.e., students in these disciplines are expected to be proficient both technically and communicatively).

Engineering is one such discipline experiencing a shift toward incorporating oral communication instruction within a highly technical curriculum (Beaufait, 1991). The 1995 report from the National Board of Engineering Education includes recommendations for a redesign of the engineering curriculum toward a more professional focus with specific attention on instruction in communication. Additionally, the Accreditation Board for Engineering and Technology (ABET) has developed new standards for accreditation to evaluate departments and colleges of engineering around the country. Specifically, ABET assessment procedures are driven by 11 student outcome measures, one of which states that students should

Publication information

Ann L. Darling (PhD, University of Washington) is Associate Professor and Chair of the Department of Communication at the University of Utah. Deanna P. Dannels (PhD, University of Utah) is Assistant Professor of Communication and Assistant Director of the Campus Writing and Speaking Program at North Carolina State University. The authors wish to thank the gracious and abundant contributions of the College of Engineering at the University of Utah, especially on the part of Professor Robert Roemer.

Communication Education, Vol. 52, No. 1, January 2003, pp. 1–16

FIRST PAGE OF ARTICLE

Darling, A. L., & Dannels, D. P. (2003). Practicing engineers talk about the importance of talk: A report on the role of oral communication in the workplace. *Communication Education, 52,* 1–16.

AUTHOR'S NAME

The author's last name comes first, followed by the author's initials.

Join two authors' names with a comma and an ampersand.

TITLE OF ARTICLE

- Do not use quotation marks. If there is a book title in the article title, italicize it.

- The first word of the title, the first word of the subtitle, and any proper nouns in the title are capitalized.

DATE OF PUBLICATION

Give the year the work was published in parentheses.

Most popular magazines are paginated per issue. These periodicals might have a volume number, but they are more often referenced by the season or date of publication.

PUBLICATION INFORMATION

Name of journal

- Italicize the journal name (or underline if you are working on a typewriter).

- All nouns, verbs, and pronouns, and the first word of the title are capitalized. Do not capitalize any article, preposition, or coordinating conjunction unless it is the first word of the title or subtitle.

- Put a comma after the journal name.

- Italicize the volume number followed by a comma.

Volume, issue, and page numbers

See sample references 26–29 for examples of different types of pagination.

Sample references for periodical sources

23. Article by one author

> Kellogg, R. T. (2001). Competition for working memory among writing processes. *American Journal of Psychology*, *114*, 175–192.

24. Article by multiple authors

> Darling, A. L., & Dannels, D. P. (2003). Practicing engineers talk about the importance of talk: A report on the role of oral communication in the workplace. *Communication Education*, *52,* 1–16.

25. Article by an unknown author

> The net is where the kids are. (2003, May 10). *Business Week*, 44.

26. Article in a journal with continuous pagination

> Engen, R., & Steen, S. (2000). The power to punish: Discretion and sentencing reform in the war on drugs. *American Journal of Sociology*, *105,* 1357–1395.

27. Article in a journal paginated by issue

> Davis, J. (1999). Rethinking globalisation. *Race and Class, 40*(2/3), 37–48.

28. Monthly publications

> Barlow, J. P. (1998, January). Africa rising: Everything you know about Africa is wrong. *Wired*, 142–158.

29. Newspaper article

> Hagenbaugh, B. (2005, April 25). Grads welcome an uptick in hiring. *USA Today*, p. A1.

15e ONLINE SOURCES IN THE APA-STYLE REFERENCES LIST

Kelty, C. (2000). *Scale, or the fact of.* Retrieved January 2, 2002, from http://kelty.org/or/papers/scaleUS.pdf

AUTHOR'S NAME, ASSOCIATED INSTITUTION, OR ORGANIZATION

- Authorship is sometimes hard to discern for online sources. If you do have an author or creator to cite, follow the rules for periodicals and books.

- If the only authority you find is a group or organization, list its name as the author.

- If the author or organization is not identified, begin the reference with the title of the document.

DATES

You need to list two dates for a Web site.

First, list the date the site was produced or last revised after the author. This date might be just a year.

Second, list the date you accessed the site. Place this second date just before the URL.

NAME OF SITE AND TITLE OF PAGE OR ARTICLE

- Web sites are often made up of many separate pages or articles. If you are citing a page or article that has a title, treat the title like an article in a periodical. Otherwise, treat the name of the Web site itself as you would a book.

- The name of a Web site will usually be found on its index or home page. If you cannot find a link back to the home page, look at the address for clues. You can work your way backward through the URL, deleting sections (separated by slashes) until you come to a home or index page.

- If there is no title for the Web site, list it by author or creator. If it is a personal home page, place the words *Home page* after the name of the owner of the page.

URL

- Copy the address exactly as it appears in your browser window.

- Note that there are no angle brackets around the URL and no period after it.

Sample references for online sources

30. Online publication by a known author

Carr, A. (2003. May 22), AAUW applauds senate support of title IX resolution. Retrieved April 1, 2004, from http://www.aauw.org/about/newsroom/press_releases/030522.cfm

31. Online publication by a group or organization

Girls Incorporated. (2003). Girls' bill of rights. Retrieved April 28, 2004, from http://www.girlsinc.org/gc/page.php?id=9

32. Article in an online scholarly journal

Brown, B. (2004). The order of service: the practical management of customer interaction. *Socological Research Online, 9*(4). Retrieved December 16, 2004, from http://www.socresonline.org.uk/ 9/4/brown.html

33. Article in an online newspaper

Slevin, C. (2005, April 25). Lawmakers want to put limits on private toll roads. *Boulder Daily Camera*. Retrieved April 25, 2005, from http://www.dailycamera.com/bdc/legislature/article/0,1713,BDC_16336_3720378,00.html

34. Article in an online magazine

Pein, C. (2005, April 20). Is Al-Jazeera ready for prime time? *Salon*. Retrieved April 25, 2005, from http://www.salon.com/news/feature/2005/04/22/aljazeera/index.html

35. Document from a database

Chandana, P. (2005). Sensorimotor control of biped locomotion. *Adaptive Behavior, 13*, 67–80. Retrieved August 22, 2005, from PsychINFO database.

36. Online government publication

U.S. Public Health Service. Office of the Surgeon General. (2001, March 11). *Women and smoking*. 15 January 2004. Retrieved April 25, 2004, from http://www.surgeongeneral.gov/library/womenandtobacco/

37. Weblog entry

Albritton, C. (2004, May 19). Greetings from Baghdad. *Back to Iraq*. Retrieved June 4, 2004, from http://www.back-to-iraq.com/

15f VISUAL, COMPUTER, AND MULTIMEDIA SOURCES IN THE APA-STYLE REFERENCES LIST

38. Television program

Burgess, M., & Green, M. (Writers). (2004). Irregular around the margins. [Television series episode]. In D. Chase (Producer), *The Sopranos*. New York: HBO.

39. Film, Video, or DVD

Columbus, C. (Director). (2001). *Harry Potter and the sorcerer's stone* [Motion picture]. United States: Warner Brothers.

40. Musical recording
In the in-text citation, include side or track numbers.

Waits, T. (1980). Ruby's arms. On *Heartattack and vine* [CD]. New York: Elektra Entertainment.

15g SAMPLE RESEARCH PAPER AND REFERENCE LIST PAGES

APA style uses a title page. ●────────●Body Objectification   1

Include page header and page number, beginning with the title page. ────── ●Running head: BODY OBJECTIFICATION

Type the running head (the shortened title) for publication in all caps, flush left.

Center the title, name of author(s), and name of school. ────●

Body Objectification: Relationship with
Fashion Magazines and Weight Satisfaction
Michael Moshenrose and Keli A. Braitman
Southern Illinois University-Carbondale

Continue to use the running head with the page number in the top right.

The abstract appears on a separate page with the title *Abstract*.

Do not indent the first line of the abstract.

Double-space the abstract.

Body Objectification   2

Abstract

This study examined the relationship between objectified body consciousness and the utilization of fashion magazines for information about fashion and beauty, comparison to models, and weight satisfaction. Participants were 180 female undergraduate students. We hypothesized that highly body-conscious individuals would read more fashion magazines than low body-conscious women and also rate magazine advertisements and articles as important for influencing fashion and beauty ideals. We also hypothesized that highly body-conscious women would compare themselves to models and be less satisfied with their weight as compared to low body-conscious women. A multivariate analysis of variance indicated that significant differences

Body Objectification   3

between the groups existed, but that group differences were opposite to hypotheses. Possible explanations for findings are discussed.

The abstract must be brief. The limit is 120 words.

Body Objectification   4

Body Objectification: Relationship with Fashion Magazines and Weight Satisfaction

Introduction

The cultural preoccupation with physical beauty has generated much research regarding how a woman's perception of her body contributes to negative body esteem. Feminist theorists argue that the female body is often treated as an object to be looked at. This objectification causes women to perceive their bodies as detached observers, which means they are attempting to see themselves as others see them. An internalization of the cultural body standards results in women believing that they created these standards and can achieve them. Therefore, objectified body consciousness (OBC) refers to perceiving the body as an object and the beliefs that sustain this perception (McKinley, 1995). McKinley and Hyde (1996) developed the 24-item

Give the full title at the beginning of the body of the report.

Center the heading *Introduction*.

Specify 1-inch margins.

Indent each paragraph five to seven spaces (1/2″ on the ruler in the word processing program).

Include the date in parentheses when you mention authors in the text.

Body Objectification   5

instrument to assess OBC, and the three scale facets are body
surveillance, control beliefs, and body shame. In order to
conform to cultural body standards, women engage in self-
surveillance to avoid negative evaluations (McKinley & Hyde,
1996). Thus, women are constantly seeing themselves as
others see them, and this act of mental disassociation can
have negative consequences for women.

Include authors and date in parentheses when you do not mention authors in the text.

. . .

Number tables and figures. Give each table and figure a descriptive title. Begin the title flush left and in italics.

Table 1

*Means and Standard Deviations for the Objectified
Body Consciousness Groups*

	Objectified Body Consciousness				
	Low (n = 25)		High (n = 31)		
Dependent Variable	M	SD	M	SD	F(1,53)
Fashion Magazines	30.12	15.40	20.65	13.67	5.26
Magazine Advertisements	18.16	4.67	12.84	4.06	19.59***
Magazine Articles	3.24	7.37	21.90	6.14	37.55***
Comparison to Models	21.72	4.84	14.13	5.85	25.82**
Weight Satisfaction	19.36	5.82	26.16	7.65	12.08**

Asterisks are normally used for notes of statistical probability.

Note. ** $p < .01$, *** $p < .001$.

. . .

Body Objectification 6

References

Akan, G. E., & Grilo, C. M. (1995). Sociocultural influences on eating attitudes and behaviors, body image, and psychological functioning: A comparison of African-American, Asian-American, and Caucasian college women. *International Journal of Eating Disorders, 18,* 181–187.

Altabe, M. N. (1998). Ethnicity and body image: Quantitative and qualitative analysis. *International Journal of Eating Disorders, 23,* 153–159.

Cash, T. F., & Henry, P. E. (1995). Women's body images: The results of a national survey in the U.S.A. *Sex Roles, 33,* 19–28.

Franzoi, S. L., & Shields, S. A. (1984). The Body Esteem Scale: Multidimensional structure and sex differences in a college population. *Journal of Personality Assessment, 48,* 173–178.

Levine, M. P., Smolak, L., & Hayden, H. (1994). The relation of sociocultural factors to eating attitudes and behaviors among middle school girls. *Journal of Early Adolescence, 14,* 471–490.

McKinley, N. M. (1995). Women and objectified body consciousness: A feminist psychological analysis. *Dissertation Abstracts International, 56,* 05B.

. . .

Center *References*.

Alphabetize entries by last name of the author.

Double-space all entries.

Indent all but the first line of each entry five spaces.

Go through your text and make sure that everything you have cited, except for personal communication, is in the list of references.

CHAPTER 16

CMS Documentation

Writers in business, social sciences, fine arts, and humanities often use the *Chicago Manual of Style* (CMS) method of documentation. CMS guidelines allow writers a clear way of using footnotes and endnotes for quotations, summaries, and paraphrases. If you have further questions, consult the complete CMS style manual, *The Chicago Manual of Style*, fifteenth edition (Chicago: University of Chicago Press, 2003).

16a THE ELEMENTS OF CMS DOCUMENTATION

CMS uses a superscript number directly after any quotation, paraphrase, or summary. Notes are numbered consecutively throughout the text. This superscript number corresponds to either a footnote, which appears at the bottom of the page, or an endnote, which appears at the end of the text.

> In *Southern Honor: Ethics and Behavior in the Old South*, Wyatt-Brown argues that "paradox, irony, and guilt have been three current words used by historians to describe white Southern life before the Civil War."[1]

Note

> 1. Bertram Wyatt-Brown, *Southern Honor: Ethics and Behavior in the Old South* (Oxford: Oxford University Press, 1983), 3.

Bibliography

> Wyatt-Brown, Bertram. *Southern Honor: Ethics and Behavior in the Old South*. Oxford: Oxford University Press, 1983.

Footnotes appear at the bottom of the page on which each citation appears. Begin your footnote four lines from the last line of text on the page. Footnotes are single-spaced, but you should double-space between notes.

Endnotes are compiled at the end of the text on a separate page entitled *Notes*. Center the title at the top of the page and list your endnotes in the order they appear within the text. The entire endnote section should be double-spaced—both within and between each entry.

Bibliography. Because footnotes and endnotes in CMS format contain complete citation information, a separate list of references is optional. This list of references can be called the *Bibliography*, or if it only has works referenced directly in your text, *Works Cited, Literature Cited,* or *References*. Generally, CMS bibliographies follow the MLA works-cited format.

See Section 16e for sample pages showing CMS research paper format.

16b BOOKS AND NONPERIODICAL SOURCES IN CMS STYLE

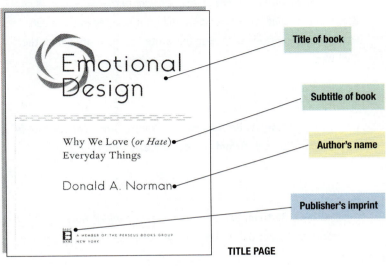

Title of book

Subtitle of book

Author's name

Publisher's imprint

TITLE PAGE

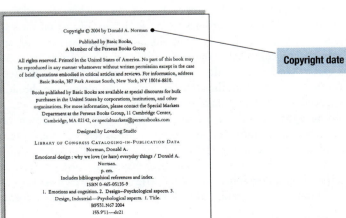

Copyright date

DETAIL OF COPYRIGHT PAGE

Note

1. Donald A. Norman, *Emotional Design: Why We Love (or Hate) Everyday Things* (New York: Basic Books, 2004), 104.

Bibliography

Norman, Donald A. *Emotional Design: Why We Love (or Hate) Everyday Things*. New York: Basic Books, 2004.

AUTHOR'S OR EDITOR'S NAME

Note: the author's name is given in normal order.

Bibliography: give the author's last name first. If an editor, put *ed.* after the name.

BOOK TITLE

Use the exact title, as it appears on the title page (not the cover).

Italicize the title.

Capitalize all nouns, verbs, adjectives, adverbs, and pronouns, and the first word of the title and subtitle.

PUBLICATION INFORMATION

In a note, the place of publication, publisher, and year of publication are in parentheses.

Place of publication

- Add the state's postal abbreviation or country when the city is not well known (*Foster City, CA*) or ambiguous (Cambridge, MA, or Cambridge, UK).

- If more than one city is given on the title page, use the first.

Publisher's name

- You may use acceptable abbreviations (e.g., Co. for Company).

- For works published prior to 1900, the place and date are sufficient.

Year of publication

- If no year of publication is given, write *n.d.* ("no date") in place of the date.

- If it is a multivolume edited work published over a period of more than one year, put the span of time as the year.

Sample citations for books and nonperiodical sources

1. Book by one author
In a note, the author's name is given in normal order.

> 1. Thomas Friedman, *The World Is Flat: A Brief History of the Twenty-first Century* (New York: Farrar, Straus, and Giroux, 2005), 9.

In subsequent references, cite the author's last name only:

> 2. Friedman, 10.

If the reference is to the same work as the reference before it, you can use the abbreviation *Ibid.*:

> 3. Ibid., 10.

In the bibliography, give the author's name in reverse order.

> Friedman, Thomas. *The World Is Flat: A Brief History of the Twenty-first Century*. New York: Farrar, Straus, and Giroux, 2005.

For edited books, put *ed.* after the name.

> Chen, Kuan-Hsing, ed. *Trajectories: Inter-Asia Cultural Studies*. London: Routledge, 1998.

2. Book by two or three authors
In a note, put all authors' names in normal order. For subsequent references, give only the authors' last names:

> 4. McClelland and Eismann, 32.

In the bibliography, give second and third authors' names in normal order.

> Hauser, Taylor, and June Kashpaw. *January Blues*. Foster City, CA: IDG Books, 2003.

3. Book by four or more authors

In a note, give the name of the first author listed, followed by *and others*.

> 5. Jacqueline Jones and others, *Created Equal: A Social and Political History of the United States* (New York: Longman, 2003), 243.

List all of the authors in the bibliography.

> Jones, Jacqueline, Peter H. Wood, Elaine Taylor May, Thomas Borstelmann, and Vicki L. Ruiz. *Created Equal: A Social and Political History of the United States*. New York: Longman, 2003.

4. Book by a group or organization

Note

> 7. World Health Organization. *Advancing Safe Motherhood through Human Rights* (Geneva, Switzerland: World Health Organization, 2001), 18.

Bibliography

> World Health Organization. *Advancing Safe Motherhood through Human Rights*. Geneva, Switzerland: World Health Organization, 2001.

5. A selection in an anthology or a chapter in an edited collection

Note

> 3. Renato Constantino, "Globalization and the South," in *Trajectories: Inter-Asia Cultural Studies*, ed. Kuan-Hsing Chen (London: Routledge, 1998), 57–64.

Bibliography

> Constantino, Renato. "Globalization and the South." In *Trajectories:
> Inter-Asia Cultural Studies*, edited by Kuan-Hsing Chen, 57–64.
> London: Routledge, 1998.

6. Government document

Note

> 5. U.S. Department of Health and Public Safety, *Grade School
> Hygiene and Epidemics* (Washington, D.C.: GPO, 1998), 21.

Bibliography

> U.S. Department of Health and Public Safety. *Grade School Hygiene
> and Epidemics*. Washington, D.C.: GPO, 1998.

7. Religious texts

Citations from religious texts appear in the notes, but not in the bibliography. Give the version in parentheses in the first citation only.

Note

> 4. John 3:16 (King James Version).

16c PERIODICAL SOURCES IN CMS STYLE

Note

1. Antoinette Galotala, "From Bohemianism to Radicalism: The Art of the *Liberator*," *American Studies International* 40 (2002): 2–32.

Bibliography

Galotala, Antoinette. "From Bohemianism to Radicalism: The Art of the *Liberator*." *American Studies International* 40 (2002): 2–32.

AUTHOR'S OR EDITOR'S NAME

Note: the author's name is given in normal order.

Bibliography: give the author's last name first.

TITLE OF ARTICLE

- Put the title in quotation marks. If there is a title of a book within the title, italicize it.
- Capitalize nouns, verbs, adjectives, adverbs, and pronouns, and the first word of the title and subtitle.

PUBLICATION INFORMATION

Name of journal

- Italicize the name of the journal.
- Journal titles are normally not abbreviated in the arts and humanities unless the title of the journal is an abbreviation (*PMLA, ELH*).

Volume, issue, and page numbers

- Place the volume number after the journal title without intervening punctuation.
- For journals that are paginated from issue to issue within a volume, do not list the issue number.
- When citing an entire article, with no page numbers, place the abbreviation *vol.* before the volume number.

Date

- The date or year of publication is given in parentheses after the volume number, or issue number, if provided.

Sample citations for periodical sources

8. Article by one author

Note

1. Sumit Guha, "Speaking Historically: The Changing Voices of Historical Narration in Western India, 1400–1900," *American Historical Review* 109 (2004): 1084–98.

Bibliography

Guha, Sumit. "Speaking Historically: The Changing Voices of Historical Narration in Western India, 1400–1900." *American Historical Review* 109 (2004): 1084–98.

9. Article by two or three authors

Note

3. Pamela R. Matthews and Mary Ann O'Farrell, "Introduction: Whose Body?" *South Central Review* 18, no. 3–4 (Fall-Winter 2001): 1–5.

Bibliography

Matthews, Pamela R., and Mary Ann O'Farrell. "Introduction: Whose Body?" *South Central Review* 18, no. 3–4 (Fall-Winter 2001): 1–5.

10. Article by more than three authors

Note

5. Thompson and others, 602.

Bibliography

Thompson, Michael J., Jorgen Christensen-Dalsgaard, Mark S. Miesch, and Juri Toomre. "The Internal Rotation of the Sun." *Annual Review of Astronomy and Astrophysics* 41 (2003): 599–643.

11. Journals paginated by volume

Note

4. Susan Welsh, "Resistance Theory and Illegitimate Reproduction," *College Composition and Communication* 52 (2001): 553–73.

Bibliography

Welsh, Susan. "Resistance Theory and Illegitimate Reproduction." *College Composition and Communication* 52 (2001): 553–73.

12. Journals paginated by issue

Note

5. Tzvetan Todorov, "The New World Disorder," *South Central Review* 19, no. 2 (2002): 28–32.

Bibliography

Todorov, Tzvetan. "The New World Disorder." *South Central Review* 19, no. 2 (2002): 28–32.

13. Weekly and biweekly magazines

Note

5. Roddy Doyle, "The Dinner," *The New Yorker*, February 5, 2001, 73.

Bibliography

Doyle, Roddy. "The Dinner." *The New Yorker*, February 5, 2001, 73.

14. Newspaper article

1. Larry Kaplow and Tasgola Karla Bruner, "U.S.: Don't Let Taliban Forces Flee," *Austin American-Statesman*, November 20, 2001, final edition, sec. A.

16d   ONLINE AND COMPUTER SOURCES IN CMS STYLE

15. Document or page from a Web site

To cite original content from within a Web site, include as many descriptive elements as you can: author of the page, title of the page, title and owner of the Web site, and the URL. Include the date accessed only if the site is time-sensitive or is frequently updated. If you cannot locate an individual author, the owner of the site can stand in for the author.

Note

> 11. Steven J. Dick, "Why We Explore," U.S. National Aeronautics and Space Administration, 2005, http://www.nasa.gov/missions/solarsystem/Why_We_13.html.

Bibliography

> Dick, Steven J. "Why We Explore." U.S. National Aeronautics and Space Administration. 2005. http://www.nasa.gov/missions/solarsystem/Why_We_13.html.

16. Online book

Note

> 12. Angelina Grimké, *Appeal to the Christian Women of the South* (New York: New York Anti-Slavery Society, 1836), http://history.furman.edu/~benson/docs/grimke2.htm.

Bibliography

> Grimké, Angelina. *Appeal to the Christian Women of the South*. New York: New York Anti-Slavery Society, 1836. http://history.furman.edu/~benson/docs/grimke2.htm.

17. Online article

Note

13. Phil Agre, "The Internet and Public Discourse," *First Monday* 3:3, March 1998, http://www.firstmonday.dk/issues/issue3_3/agre/.

Bibliography

Agre, Phil. "The Internet and Public Discourse." *First Monday* 3:3, March 1998. http://www.firstmonday.dk/issues/issue3_3/agre/.

18. Documents and articles retrieved from database services

To cite documents or articles obtained through an Internet database, follow the CMS model for citing journal articles. In addition, add the URL for the main home page of the service.

Note

15. Bill T. Jones, "Tupac Shakur and the (Queer) Art of Death," *Callaloo* 23, no. 1 (2000): 384–393. http://www.jstor.org/.

Bibliography

Jones, Bill T. "Tupac Shakur and the (Queer) Art of Death." *Callaloo* 23, no. 1 (2000): 384–393. http://www.jstor.org/.

16e SAMPLE RESEARCH PAPER PAGES

1

Jason Laker

American History 102

January 9, 2002

The Electoral College: Does It Have a Future?

Until the presidential election of 2000, few Americans
thought much about the Electoral College. It was something
they had learned about in civics class and had then forgotten
about as other, more pressing bits of information required
their attention. In November 2000, however, the Electoral
College took center stage and sparked an argument that
continues today: Should the Electoral College be abolished?

The founding fathers established the Electoral College as
a compromise between elections by Congress and those by
popular vote.[1] The College consists of a group of electors
who meet to vote for the president and vice president of the
United States. The electors are nominated by political parties
within each state and the number each state gets relates to
the state's congressional delegation.[2] The process and the
ideas behind it sound simple, but the actual workings of the
Electoral College remain a mystery to many Americans.

The complicated nature of the Electoral College is one
of the reasons why some people want to see it abolished.

. . .

Notes

1. Lawrence D. Longley and Neal R. Peirce, *The Electoral College Primer 2000* (New Haven: Yale University Press, 1999).

2. Office of the Federal Register, "A Procedural Guide to the Electoral College," Electoral College Home page, http://www.nara.gov/fedreg/elctcoll/proced.html.

3. William C. McIntyre, "Revisiting the Electoral College," *New York Times,* November 17, 2001, late edition, sec. A.

4. Avagara, *EC: The Electoral College Webzine,* http://www.avagara.com/e_c/.

5. Gary Gregg, "Keep the College," *National Review Online,* November 7, 2001, http://www.lexisnexis.com/universe/.

. . .

5

Bibliography

Avagara. *EC: The Electoral College Webzine*.
     http://www.avagara.com/e_c/.
Gregg, Gary. "Keep the College." *National Review Online*,
     November 7, 2001. http://www.lexisnexis.com/
     universe/.

. . .

CHAPTER 17
CSE Documentation

In the natural and applied sciences, citation styles are highly specialized. The Council of Science Editors (CSE) publishes *Scientific Style and Format: The CBE Manual for Authors, Editors, and Publishers,* sixth edition (1994). Additional information on CSE style can be found online at http://www.councilscienceeditors.org/publications/ssf_7th.cfm.

17a THE ELEMENTS OF CSE DOCUMENTATION

CSE style allows writers two alternative methods for documenting sources: the **name-year system** and the **citation-sequence system.** In the CSE name-year system, both the author's last name and the year of publication appear together in parentheses directly following cited material in the text.

> The Red-cockaded Woodpecker (*Picoides borealis*) typically uses a single cavity for nesting (Ligon 1970, Walters et al. 1988).

In the CSE citation-sequence system, citations in the body of the text are marked by a superscript number placed inside punctuation. For example,

> Cold fingers and toes are common circulatory problems found in most heavy cigarette smokers[1].

This number corresponds to a numbered entry on the CSE source list, titled *References*.

To create a CSE References page, follow these guidelines:

1. Title your page "References," and center this title at the top of the page.
2. Double-space the entire References page, both within and between citations.
3. For papers using the **citation-sequence system,** list citations in the order they appear in the body of the paper. Begin each citation with its citation number, followed by a period, flush left.
4. For papers using the **name-year system,** list references, unnumbered, in alphabetical order. Begin each citation flush left. Indent any subsequent lines of the citation five spaces.

17b IN-TEXT CITATIONS IN CSE STYLE

> **Name-year system (N-Y)**
> In 1997, the Gallup poll reported that 55% of adults in the United States think secondhand smoke is "very harmful," compared to only 36% in 1994 (Saad 2000).

Citation-sequence system (C-S)

In 1997, the Gallup poll reported that 55% of adults in the United States think secondhand smoke is "very harmful," compared to only 36% in 1994[1].

The superscript [1] refers to the first entry on the References list, where readers will find a complete citation for this source.

Sample in-text citations (name-year system)

1. Work by a one author

(Barron 2001)

2. Work by two authors

(Monastersky and Allen 1998)

If the authors have the same last name, add their initials.

(Allen SR and Allen TJ 1997)

3. Work by three or more authors

(Barker and others 1972)

4. Work by a group or organization

Treat the group or organization as the author.

(WHO 2001)

17c   BOOKS AND NONPERIODICAL SOURCES IN CSE-STYLE REFERENCES

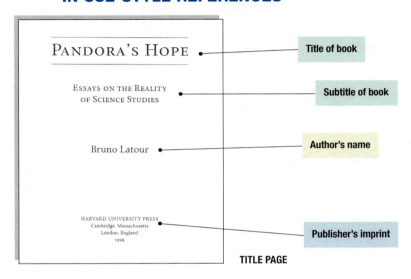

PANDORA'S HOPE   •——— **Title of book**

ESSAYS ON THE REALITY
OF SCIENCE STUDIES •——— **Subtitle of book**

Bruno Latour •——— **Author's name**

HARVARD UNIVERSITY PRESS
Cambridge, Massachusetts
London, England •——— **Publisher's imprint**
1999

TITLE PAGE

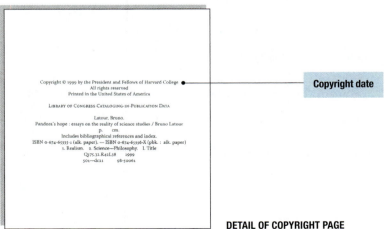

Copyright © 1999 by the President and Fellows of Harvard College •——— **Copyright date**
All rights reserved
Printed in the United States of America

LIBRARY OF CONGRESS CATALOGING-IN-PUBLICATION DATA

Latour, Bruno.
Pandora's hope : essays on the reality of science studies / Bruno Latour
p.   cm.
Includes bibliographical references and index.
ISBN 0-674-65335-1 (alk. paper). — ISBN 0-674-65336-X (pbk. : alk. paper)
1. Realism.   2. Science—Philosophy.   I. Title
Q175.32.R42L38   1999
501—dc21   98-50061

DETAIL OF COPYRIGHT PAGE

Name-Year (N-Y)

Latour B. 1999. Pandora's hope: essays on the reality of science studies. Cambridge: Harvard Univ Pr. 324 p.

Citation-Sequence (C-S)

1. Latour B. Pandora's hope: essays on the reality of science studies. Cambridge: Harvard Univ Pr; 1999. 324 p.

AUTHOR'S OR EDITOR'S NAME

The author's last name comes first, followed by the initials of the author's first name and middle name (if provided). If an editor, put the word *editor* after the name.

BOOK TITLE

- Do not italicize or underline titles.
- Capitalize only the first word and proper nouns.

PUBLICATION INFORMATION

Year of publication

- In **N-Y**, the year comes after the author(s). In **C-S**, the year comes after the other publication information. It follows a semicolon.
- If it is a multivolume edited work, published over a period of more than 1 year, give the span of years.

Page numbers

- When citing an entire book, give the total number of pages: *324 p.*
- When citing part of a book, give the page range for the selection: *p. 60–90.*

Sample references for books and nonperiodical sources in CSE style

5. Book by one author/editor

The author's last name comes first, followed by the initials of the author's first name and middle name (if provided). If an editor, put the word *editor* after the name.

N-Y   Minger TJ, editor. 1990. Greenhouse glasnost: the crisis of global warming. New York: Ecco. 292 p.

C-S   2. Minger T, editor. Greenhouse glasnost: the crisis of global warming. New York: Ecco; 1990. 292 p.

6. Book by two or more authors/editors

N-Y   O'Day DH, Horgen PA, editors. 1981. Sexual interactions in eukaryotic microbes. New York: Academic. 407 p.

C-S   3. O'Day DH, Horgen PA, editors. Sexual interactions in eukaryotic microbes. New York: Academic; 1981. 407 p.

7. Book by a group or organization

In N-Y, the full name is given, preceded by the abbreviation, in brackets.

N-Y   [IAEA] International Atomic Energy Association. 1971. Manual on radiation haematology. Vienna: IAEA. 430 p.

C-S   4. IAEA. Manual on radiation haematology. Vienna: IAEA; 1971. 430 p.

8. Two or more books by the same author

In C-S, number the references according to the order in which they appear in the text. In N-Y, arrange them by date, or alphabetically according to names of additional authors. If the date and the additional authors are the same, arrange according to title. To clarify in-text citation, assign a letter (a, b, c) to the repeated dates.

> Clarke JJ. 1903a. Protozoa and disease. New York: W Wood.
>
> Clarke JJ. 1903b. Rhizopod protozoa. New York: W Wood.

9. A selection in an anthology or a chapter in an edited collection

The author of the selection is listed first. The year given is for the collection. Put the word *In* and a colon before the editor of the collection.

> **N-Y** Kraft K, Baines DM. 1997. Computer classrooms and third grade development. In: Green MD, editor. Computers and early development. New York: Academic. p. 168-79.
>
> **C-S** 7. Kraft K, Baines DM. Computer classrooms and third grade development. In: Green MD, editor. Computers and early development. New York: Academic; 1997. p. 168-79.

17d PERIODICAL SOURCES IN CSE-STYLE REFERENCES

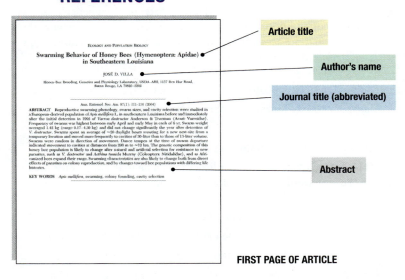

Article title

Author's name

Journal title (abbreviated)

Abstract

FIRST PAGE OF ARTICLE

Text of article

Name-Year (N-Y)

Villa JD. 2005. Swarming behavior of honey bees (*Hymenoptera: Apidae*) in southeastern Louisiana. Ann. Entomol. Soc. Am. 97:111-6.

Citation-Sequence (C-S)

1. Villa JD. Swarming behavior of honey bees (*Hymenoptera: Apidae*) in southeastern Louisiana. Ann. Entomol. Soc. Am. 2004; 97:111-6.

AUTHOR'S NAME

The author's last name comes first, followed by the initials of the author's first name and middle name (if provided).

TITLE OF ARTICLE

- Do not italicize or underline titles.
- Capitalize only the first word and proper nouns.

PUBLICATION INFORMATION

Name of journal

- Do not abbreviate single-word titles. Abbreviate multiple-word titles according to the National Information Standards Organization (NISO) list of serials.
- Capitalize the journal title, even if abbreviated.

Date of publication, volume, and issue numbers

- For continuously paginated journals, include only the year and volume number, not the issue number.

Sample references for periodical sources in CSE style

10. Article by one author

N-Y　Board J. 2001. Reduced lodging for soybeans in low plant
　　　population is related to light quality. Crop Science 41:379-87.

C-S　1. Board J. Reduced lodging for soybeans in low plant population
　　　is related to light quality. Crop Science 2001; 41:379-87.

11. Article by two or more authors/editors

N-Y　Simms K, Denison D. 1997. Observed interactions between wild
　　　and domesticated mixed-breed canines. J. Mamm 70:341-2.

C-S　2. Simms K, Denison D. Observed interactions between wild and
　　　domesticated mixed-breed canines. J. Mamm 1997; 70:341-2.

12. Article by a group or organization

N-Y　[CSPI] Center for Science in the Public Interest. 2001 Apr 1.
　　　Meat labeling: help! Nutrition Action Health Letter: 2.

17e ONLINE SOURCES IN CSE-STYLE REFERENCES

Name-year (N-Y)

Lowe C. 2001. Speech recognition: sci-fi or composition? Currents in
　　Electronic Literacy [serial online]. 4. Available from:
　　http://www.cwrl.utexas.edu/ currents/archives/spr01/
　　lowe.html. Accessed 2001 June 10.

Citation-sequence (C-S)

1. Lowe C. Speech recognition: sci-fi or composition? Currents in
　　Electronic Literacy [serial online] 2001;4. Available from:
　　http://www.cwrl.utexas.edu/currents/archives/spr01/lowe.html.
　　Accessed 2001 June 10.

PART FOUR

Style and Language

18 WRITE WITH POWER

a   Recognize active and passive voice
b   Use action verbs
c   Name your agents
d   Vary your sentences

19 WRITE CONCISELY

a   Eliminate unnecessary words
b   Reduce wordy phrases
c   Simplify tangled sentences

20 WRITE WITH EMPHASIS

a   Manage emphasis within sentences
b   Forge links across sentences
c   Use parallel structure with parallel ideas

21 FIND THE RIGHT WORDS

a   Recognize varieties of English
b   Be aware of levels of formality
c   Be aware of denotation and connotation
d   Use specific language
e   Write to be inclusive

CHAPTER 18
Write with Power

Keeping a few principles in mind can make your writing a pleasure to read instead of a chore.

In photographs

Viewers imagine actions when subjects are captured in motion.

In writing

Readers expect actions to be expressed in verbs:
gallop, canter, trot, run, sprint, dash, bound, thunder, tear away

In photographs

Viewers interpret the most prominent person or thing as the subject—what the photograph is about.

In writing

Readers interpret the first person or thing they meet in a sentence as what the sentence is about (the jockey, the horse). They expect that person or thing to do the action expressed in the verb.

18a RECOGNIZE ACTIVE AND PASSIVE VOICE

In the **active voice** the subject of the sentence is the actor. In the **passive voice** the subject is being acted upon.

ACTIVE   **Leonardo da Vinci painted** *Mona Lisa* between 1503 and 1506.

PASSIVE   ***Mona Lisa* was painted** by Leonardo da Vinci between 1503 and 1506.

To write with power, use the active voice. Observe the difference:

PASSIVE The pear tree in the front yard **was demolished** by the un-expected storm.

ACTIVE The unexpected storm **demolished** the pear tree in the front yard.

18b USE ACTION VERBS

Where are the action words in the following sentences?

> The 1980 Olympic games were in Moscow. Two months before the start of the Olympics was the Soviet invasion of Afghanistan. President Jimmy Carter was unhappy about the Soviet invasion and other allies were in sympathy.

No action words here! The passage describes a series of actions, yet the only verbs are forms of *be (was, were)*. Think about what the actions are and choose powerful verbs that express those actions.

> Just two months before the 1980 Olympic games were to be held in Moscow, the Soviet Union **invaded** Afghanistan. President Jimmy Carter **denounced** the invasion and **declared** an American boycott of the Olympics.

Many sentences contain words that express action, but those words are nouns instead of verbs. Often the nouns can be changed into verbs. For example:

> The arson unit ~~conducted an investigation of~~ **investigated** the myste-rious fire.

> The committee ~~had a debate over~~ **debated** how best to spend the sur-plus funds.

Notice that changing nouns into verbs also eliminates unnecessary words.

18c NAME YOUR AGENTS

The **agent** is the person or thing that does the action. Powerful writing puts the agents in sentences.

Include people

Read the following sentence aloud:

> The use of a MIDI keyboard for playing the song will facilitate capturing it in digital form on our laptop for the subsequent purpose of uploading it to our Web site.

It sounds dead, doesn't it? Putting people into the sentence makes it come alive:

> By playing the song on a MIDI keyboard, **we** can record the digitized sound on our laptop and then upload it to our Web site.

Including people makes your writing more emphatic. Most readers relate better to people than to abstractions. Putting people in your sentences also introduces active verbs because people do things.

Focus on your agents

Even when you are not writing about people, keep the focus on your agents. Read this short section from a report written by an engineer who was asked to recommend which of two types of valves an oil company should purchase for one of its refineries.

> Although the two systems function similarly, Farval valves have two distinct advantages. First, Farval grease valves include a pin indicator that shows whether the valve is working. Alemite valves must be checked by taking them apart. Second, Farval valves have metal seals, while Alemite valves have rubber grommet seals. If an Alemite valve fails, the pressure will force grease past the rubber grommet seals, creating a grease puddle on the floor. By contrast, Farval's metal seals contain the grease if the valve fails.

This engineer not only makes a definite recommendation supported by reasons, she also makes her report easy to read by keeping the focus on the two types of valves she is comparing.

18d VARY YOUR SENTENCES

Read the following passage.

> On the first day Garth, Jim, and I paddled fourteen miles down Johnstone Strait. We headed down the strait about five more miles to Robson Bight. It is a famous scratching place for orcas. The Bight is a small bay. We paddled out into the strait so we could see the entire Bight. There were no orcas inside. By this time we were getting tired. We were hungry. The clouds assumed a wintry dark thickness. The wind was kicking up against us. Our heads were down going into the cold spray.

The subject matter is interesting, but the writing isn't. The passage is a series of short sentences, one after the other. When you have too many short sentences one after the other, try combining a few of them.

The result of combining some (but not all) short sentences is a paragraph whose sentences match the interest of the subject.

> On the first day Garth, Jim, and I paddled fourteen miles down Johnstone Strait. We headed down the strait about five more miles to Robson Bight, a small bay known as a famous scratching place for orcas. We paddled out into the strait so we could see the entire Bight, but there were no orcas inside. By this time we were tired and hungry, the clouds had assumed a wintry dark thickness, and the wind was kicking up against us—our heads dropped going into the cold spray.

 C H A P T E R 1 9

Write Concisely

Clutter creeps into our lives every day. Clutter also creeps into writing through unnecessary words, inflated constructions, and excessive jargon.

In regards to the Web site, the content is **pretty** successful **in consideration of** the topic. The site is **fairly** good writing-wise and is **very** unique in telling you how to adjust the rear derailleur one step at a time.

The words in **red** are clutter. Get rid of the clutter. You can say the same thing with half the words and gain more impact as a result.

The well-written Web site on bicycle repair provides step-by-step instructions on adjusting your rear derailleur.

19a ELIMINATE UNNECESSARY WORDS

Empty words resemble the foods that add calories without nutrition. Put your writing on a diet.

Redundancy

Some words act as modifiers, but when you look closely at them, they repeat the meaning of the word they pretend to modify. Have you heard someone refer to a *personal friend*? Aren't all friends personal? Likewise, you may have heard expressions such as *red in color, small in size, round in shape,* or *honest truth.* Imagine *red* not referring to color or *round* not referring to shape.

19b REDUCE WORDY PHRASES

Many inexperienced writers use phrases like "It is my opinion that" or "I think that" to begin sentences. These phrases are deadly to read. If you find them in your prose, cut them. Unless a writer is citing a source, we assume that the ideas are the writer's.

Coaches are among the worst at using many words for what could be said in a few:

After much deliberation about Brown's future in football with regard to possible permanent injuries, I came to the conclusion that it would be in his best interest not to continue his pursuit of playing football again.

The coach might have said simply:

> Because Brown risks permanent injury if he plays football again, I decided to release him from the team.

Perhaps the coach wanted to sound impressive, authoritative, or thoughtful. But the result is the opposite. Speakers and writers who impress us are those who use words efficiently.

COMMON ERRORS

Empty intensifiers

Intensifiers modify verbs, adjectives, and other adverbs, and they often are overused. One of the most overused intensifiers is *very*. Take the following sentence as an example:

> Her clothing style was **very unique**.

If something is unique, it is one of a kind. The word *very* doesn't make something more than unique.

> Her clothing style was **unique**.

Or

> Her clothing style was **strange**.

Very and *totally* are but two of a list of empty intensifiers that usually can be eliminated with no loss of meaning. Other empty intensifiers include *absolutely, awfully, definitely, incredibly, particularly,* and *really*.

Remember: When you use *very*, *totally*, or another intensifier before an adjective or adverb, always ask yourself whether there is a more accurate adjective or adverb you could use to express the same thought.

Wordy phrases

Certain stock phrases plague writing in the workplace, in the media, and in academia. Many can be replaced by one or two words with no loss in meaning.

Wordy	Concise
at this point in time	now
due to the fact that	because
for the purpose of	for
have the ability to	can
in order to	to
in spite of the fact that	although
in the event that	if
met with her approval	she approved

19c SIMPLIFY TANGLED SENTENCES

Long sentences can be graceful and forceful. Such sentences, however, often require several revisions before they achieve elegance. Too often long sentences reflect wandering thoughts that the writer did not bother to go back and sort out. Two of the most important strategies for untangling long sentences are described in Chapter 18: using active verbs (Section 18b) and naming your agents (Section 18c). Here are some other strategies.

Revise expletives

Expletives are empty words that can occupy the subject position in a sentence. The most frequently used expletives are *there is, there are,* and *it is.*

> WORDY   **There were** several important differences between the positions raised by the candidates in the debate.

To simplify the sentence, find the agent and make it the subject.

> REVISED   The two **candidates** raised several important differences between their positions in the debate.

A few kinds of sentences—for example, *It is raining*—do require you to use an expletive. In most cases, however, expletives add unnecessary words, and sentences usually read better without them.

Use positive constructions

Sentences become wordy and hard to read if they include two or more negatives such as the words *no, not,* and *nor,* and the prefixes *un-* and *mis-*. For example:

> **DIFFICULT** A **not un**common complaint among employers of new college graduates is that they can**not** communicate effectively in writing.
>
> **REVISED** Employers frequently complain that new college graduates cannot write effectively.
>
> **EVEN SIMPLER** Employers value the rare college graduate who can write well.

Phrasing sentences positively usually makes them more economical. Moreover, it makes your style more forceful and direct.

Simplify sentence structure

Long sentences can be hard to read, not because they are long but because they are convoluted and hide the relationships among ideas. Take the following sentence as an example.

> When the cessation of eight years of hostility in the Iran–Iraq war occurred in 1988, it was not the result of one side defeating the other but the exhaustion of both after losing thousands of people and much of their military capability.

This sentence is hard to read. To rewrite sentences like this one, find the main ideas, then determine the relationships among them.

After examining the sentence, you decide there are two key ideas:

1. **Iran and Iraq stopped fighting in 1988 after eight years.**
2. **Both sides were exhausted from losing people and equipment.**

Next ask what the relationship is between the two ideas. When you identify the key ideas, the relationship is often obvious; in this case (2) is the cause of (1). Thus the word you want to connect the two ideas is *because*.

> **Iran and Iraq stopped fighting after eight years** of an indecisive war **because** **both sides had lost thousands of people and most of their equipment**.

The revised sentence is both clearer and more concise, reducing the number of words from forty-two to twenty-five.

CHAPTER 20
Write with Emphasis

Photographs and writing gain energy when key ideas are emphasized.

In visuals

Photographers create emphasis by composing the image to direct the attention of the viewer. Putting people and objects in the foreground and making them stand out against the background gives them emphasis.

In writing

Writers have many tools for creating emphasis. Writers can design a page to gain emphasis by using headings, white space, type size, color, and boldfacing. Just as important, learning the craft of structuring sentences will empower you to give your writing emphasis.

20a MANAGE EMPHASIS WITHIN SENTENCES

Put your main ideas in main clauses

Placing more important information in main clauses and less important information in subordinate clauses emphasizes what is important.

In the following paragraph all the sentences are main clauses:

> Lotteries were common in the United States before and after the American Revolution. They eventually ran into trouble. They were run by private companies. Sometimes the companies took off with the money. They didn't pay the winners.

This paragraph is grammatically correct, but it does not help the reader understand which pieces of information the author wants to emphasize. Combining the simple sentences into main and subordinate clauses and phrases can significantly improve the paragraph.

First, identify the main ideas:

> Lotteries were common in the United States before and after the American Revolution. They eventually ran into trouble.

These ideas can be combined into one sentence:

> Lotteries were common in the United States before and after the American Revolution, but they eventually ran into trouble.

Now think about the relationship of the three remaining sentences to the main ideas. Those sentences explain why lotteries ran into trouble; thus the relationship is *because*.

> Lotteries were common in the United States before and after the American Revolution, but they eventually ran into trouble **because** they were run by private companies that sometimes took off with the money instead of paying the winners.

Put key ideas at the beginning and end of sentences

Read these sentences aloud:

1   *Rain Man* and *Born on the Fourth of July*, films marking the actor's transition from teen idol to adult actor, starred **Tom Cruise**.

2   Films such as *Rain Man* and *Born on the Fourth of July*, both featuring **Tom Cruise**, helped the actor make the difficult transition from teen idol to adult actor.

3   **Tom Cruise** made the difficult transition from teen idol to adult actor, starring in films such as *Rain Man* and *Born on the Fourth of July*.

Most readers put the most emphasis on the words at the beginning and end of a sentence. This means that information in the middle of a sentence can sometimes get lost. Sentence 1 lends emphasis to the fact that these two films starred Tom Cruise. Sentence 2 emphasizes that these two films in particular helped Cruise make a transition from teen idol to serious actor. Sentence 3 puts the emphasis on the titles of the two films. Which one you choose depends on your purpose. Put new and important information at the end of a sentence.

20b FORGE LINKS ACROSS SENTENCES

When your writing maintains a focus of attention across sentences, the reader can distinguish the important ideas and how they relate to each other. To achieve this coherence, you need to control which ideas occupy the positions of greatest emphasis. The words you repeat from sentence to sentence act as links.

Link sentences from front to front

In front-to-front linkage, the subject of the sentence remains the focus from one sentence to the next. In the following sequence, sentences 1 through 5 are all about Tom Cruise. The subject of each sentence refers to the first sentence with the pronouns *he* and *his*.

1   **Tom Cruise** was born Thomas Cruise Mapother IV on July 3, 1962.

2   He struggled through school, suffering from untreated dyslexia.

3   After a high school knee injury ended his wrestling career, **his** attentions turned to acting.

4   **He** started his motion picture career in films such as *Taps* and *The Outsiders*.

5   **His** career really took off in 1983 with his iconic air guitar performance in *Risky Business*.

Each sentence adds more information about the repeated topic, Tom Cruise.

Link sentences from back to front

In back-to-front linkage, the new information at the end of the sentence is used as the topic of the next sentence. Back-to-front linkage allows new material to be introduced and commented on.

1   Tom Cruise's career really took off in 1983 with his iconic air guitar performance in ***Risky Business***.

2   **The film** simultaneously popularized Cruise and **Ray Ban Wayfarer sunglasses**.

3   **Ray Ban Wayfarers** would skyrocket in popularity, with Bausch & Lomb selling 360,000 pair in 1983 alone.

Back-to-front linkage is useful when ideas need to be advanced quickly, as when you are telling stories. Rarely, however, will you use either front-to-front linkage or back-to-front linkage continuously throughout a piece of writing. Use front-to-front linkage to add more information and back-to-front linkage to move the topic along.

Check the links between your sentences to find any gaps that will cause your readers to stumble.

20c   USE PARALLEL STRUCTURE WITH PARALLEL IDEAS

What if Patrick Henry wrote "Give me liberty or I prefer not to live"? Would we remember those words today? We do remember the words he did use: "Give me liberty or give me death." Writers who use parallel structure often create memorable sentences.

Use parallelism with coordinating conjunctions

When you join elements at the same level with coordinating conjunctions, including *and, or, nor, yet, so, but,* and *for,* normally you should use parallel grammatical structure for these elements.

> **AWKWARD**
>
> In today's global economy, **the method of production and where factories are located** has become relatively unimportant in comparison to **the creation of new concepts and marketing those concepts.**

> **PARALLEL**
>
> In today's global economy, **how goods are made and where they are produced** has become relatively unimportant in comparison to **creating new concepts and marketing those concepts.**

Use parallelism with correlative conjunctions

Make identical in structure the parts of sentences linked by correlative conjunctions: *either . . . or, neither . . . nor, not only . . . but also, whether . . . or.*

> **AWKWARD**
>
> Purchasing the undeveloped land **not only gives us a new park** but also **is something that our children will benefit from in the future.**

> **PARALLEL**
>
> Purchasing the undeveloped land **not only will give our city a new park** but also **will leave our children a lasting inheritance.**

The more structural elements you match, the stronger the effect the parallelism will achieve.

COMMON ERRORS

Faulty parallel structure

When writers neglect to use parallel structure, the result can be jarring. Reading your writing aloud will help you catch problems in parallelism. Read this sentence aloud:

> At our club meeting we identified problems in **finding** new members, **publicizing** our activities, and **maintenance** of our Web site.

The end of the sentence does not sound right because the parallel structure is broken. We expect to find another verb + *ing* following *finding* and *publicizing*. Instead, we run into *maintenance,* a noun. The problem is easy to fix: Change the noun to the *-ing* verb form.

> At our club meeting we identified problems in finding new members, publicizing our activities, and **maintaining** our Web site.

Remember: Use parallel structure for parallel elements within a sentence.

 C H A P T E R 2 1

Find the Right Words

Suppose you want to email a friend about a new song you heard on the radio. You might be impressed by the words, which you praise to your friend. Now imagine in your English class you are asked to find an example of common poetry, such as song lyrics or an advertising jingle, and to describe that poetry. You realize the song you like will fulfill the assignment and you write about the lyrics. The language you use in each case will likely be very different.

In the email to your friend, you might use contractions and slang to describe the music. In the college assignment, and in most workplace writing, you will probably use what writers call edited American English.

21a RECOGNIZE VARIETIES OF ENGLISH

As a general concept, **edited American English** is a dialect that is used in most academic, business, and public contexts. We use this dialect when we wish to be understood by the widest possible audience. That goal requires that we eliminate, or at least explain, words that have particular meanings for particular groups, and especially words that are used only by certain groups. You will write most of your college essays in edited American English, the variety of English that is best suited for a broad university audience in the United States.

Jargon

Jargon is the specialized language of a discipline or occupation. Using jargon in appropriate situations can be an effective way to communicate. When you start a new job or a new class, you often must learn a new jargon—words specific to a particular activity or field of study.

Your decision about when to use discipline-specific language in place of words a general audience would understand will depend on your audience. A doctor can say to another doctor, "The x-rays show a fracture in the fifth metatarsal." But a patient might prefer that the doctor say, "Your foot is broken." Jargon is often the most efficient and precise way for experts in a field to communicate. However, to a nonexpert audience, jargon may sound self-important if common language would do just as well. Avoid using jargon when writing to nonexpert readers. An exception is when your audience needs to learn important key terms. In these cases, be sure to define the specialized terms that your readers may not know.

Euphemisms

Euphemisms are rephrasings of harsh terms; they attempt to avoid offending or to skirt an unpleasant issue. For instance, the Federal Reserve Board is fond of calling a bad market "a market imbalance." A well-chosen euphemism can be tactful in a sensitive situation. A bereaved person might rather hear, "I was sorry to hear of your grandmother's passing" than "I was sorry to hear your grandmother died." However, poorly chosen euphemisms can hurt a writer's ethos if they are used to make excuses or downplay the sufferings of others.

21b BE AWARE OF LEVELS OF FORMALITY

While you may get plenty of practice in informal writing—emails and notes to friends and family members—mastering formal writing is essential in academic and professional settings. How formal or informal should your writing be? That depends on your audience and the writing task at hand.

Decide how formal your writing should be

- Who is your audience?
- What is the occasion?
- What level of formality is your audience accustomed to in similar situations?
- What impression of yourself do you want to give?

Colloquialisms

Colloquialisms are words or expressions that are used informally, often in conversation but less often in writing.

> I'm not happy with my grades, but that's the way **the cookie crumbles**.

> Liz is always **running at the mouth** about something.

> Caroline really **worships the ground Sharon walks on**.

> I enjoyed the restaurant, but it was **nothing to write home about**.

> I think Sue **got up on the wrong side of the bed** today.

In academic and professional writing, colloquialisms often suggest a flippant attitude, carelessness, or even thoughtlessness. Sometimes colloquialisms can be used for ironic or humorous effect, but as a general rule, if you want to be taken seriously, avoid using them.

Avoiding colloquialisms does not mean, however, that you should use big words when small ones will do as well, or that you should use ten words instead of two. Formality does not mean being pretentious or wordy.

WORDY

In this writer's opinion, one could argue that the beaches on the west coast of Florida are far superior in every particular to their counterparts on the east coast.

BETTER

I think Florida's west coast beaches are better in every way than those on the east coast.

Slang

The most conspicuous kind of language that is usually avoided in formal writing is slang. The next time a friend talks to you, listen closely to the words he or she uses. Chances are you will notice several words that you probably would not use in a college writing assignment. Slang words are created by and for a particular group—even if that group is just you and your friend.

The new iPod nano is just **the bomb**.

Joey's new **ride** is totally **pimped out**.

Slang is used to indicate membership in a particular group, and usually to avoid others. Slang excludes readers who are not part of the group, and for that reason it is best avoided in academic writing.

21c BE AWARE OF DENOTATION AND CONNOTATION

Words have both literal meanings, called **denotations**, and associated meanings, called **connotations**. The contrast is evident in words that mean roughly the same thing but have different connotations. For example, some people are set in their opinions, a quality that can be described positively as *persistent, firm,* and *steadfast* or negatively as *stubborn, bull-headed,* and *close-minded. Persistent, firm,* and *steadfast* denote someone who is not easily influenced by pressure or opinions. *Stubborn, bull-headed,* and *close-minded* can also denote someone who does not easily change his mind, but the connotative meanings are almost entirely negative. All three words carry connotations of brutishness and lack of consideration for others.

In college and professional writing, writers are expected not to rely on the connotations of words to make important points. For example, the statement *It's only common sense to have good schools* carries high positive connotations. Most people believe in common sense, and most people want good schools. What is common sense for one person, however, is not common sense for another; how a good school is defined varies greatly. This statement would not constitute an effective argument in college writing because it relies heavily on connotation in place of persuasive evidence and effective support.

21d USE SPECIFIC LANGUAGE

Be precise

Effective writing conveys information clearly and precisely. Words such as *situation, sort, thing, aspect,* and *kind* often signal undeveloped or even lazy thinking.

VAGUE	The movie was sort of a documentary-like thing.
BETTER	The movie resembled a documentary.
VAGUE	Joe DiMaggio's hitting streak lasted many games.
BETTER	Joe DiMaggio's hitting streak lasted fifty-six games.

When citing numbers or quantities, be as exact as possible. A precise number, if known, is always better than slippery words like *several* or *many,* which some writers use to cloak the fact that they don't know the quantity in question.

Use a dictionary

There is no greater tool for writers than the dictionary. Always have a dictionary handy when you write—either a book or an online version—and get into the habit of using it. In addition to checking spelling, you can find additional meanings of a word that perhaps you had not considered, and you can find the etymology—the origins of a word. In many cases knowing the etymology of a word can help you use it to better effect. For example, if you want to argue that universities as institutions have succeeded because they bring people together in contexts that prepare them for their lives after college, you might point out the etymology of *university*. *University* can be traced back to the late Latin word *universitas,* which means "society or guild," thus emphasizing the idea of a community of learning.

21e   WRITE TO BE INCLUSIVE

While the conventions of inclusiveness change continually, three guidelines for inclusive language toward all groups remain constant:

- Do not point out people's differences unless those differences are relevant to your argument.
- Call people whatever they prefer to be called.
- When given a choice of terms, choose the more accurate one. (*Vietnamese,* for example, is preferable to *Asian.*)

Be inclusive about gender

Don't use masculine nouns and pronouns to refer to both men and women. *He, his, him, man,* and *mankind* are outmoded and inaccurate terms for both genders. Eliminate gender bias by using the following tips:

- Don't say *boy* when you can say *child.*
- Use *men and women* or *people* instead of *man.*
- Use *humanity* or *humankind* in place of *mankind.*

Eliminating *he, his,* and *him* when referring to both men and women is more complicated. Many readers consider *he/she* to be an awkward alternative. Try one of the following instead:

- Make the noun and its corresponding pronoun plural. The pronoun will change from *he, him,* or *his* to *they, them,* or *theirs.*

BIASED MASCULINE PRONOUNS

An undercover agent won't reveal **his** identity, even to other agents, if **he** thinks it will jeopardize the case.

BETTER

Undercover agents won't reveal **their** identities, even to other agents, if **they** think it will jeopardize the case.

- Replace the pronoun with an article (*the*, *a*, or *an*)

BIASED MASCULINE PRONOUN

Each prospective driving instructor must pass a state test before receiving **his** license.

BETTER

Each prospective driving instructor must pass a state test before receiving **a** license.

Professional titles that indicate gender—*chairman, waitress*—falsely imply that the gender of the person doing the job changes the essence of the job being done. Use gender-neutral terms for professions. *Chair* and *server* are common gender-neutral alternatives to *chairman* and *waitress*. Likewise, avoid adding a gender designation to a gender-neutral professional title. Terms like *woman doctor* and *male nurse* imply that a woman working as a doctor and a man working as a nurse are abnormal. Instead, write simply *doctor* and *nurse*.

Be inclusive about race and ethnicity

Use the terms for racial and ethnic groups that the groups use for themselves. Use *black* to write about members of the Black Coaches' Association and *African American* to write about members of the Society for African American Brotherhood.

If you are still in doubt, err on the side of specificity. For instance, while *Latino(a), Hispanic,* and *Chicano(a)* are all frequently accepted terms for many people, choosing a term that identifies a specific country (*Mexican* or *Puerto Rican*) would be more accurate. When discussing an American's heritage, often the best term to use is the country of origin plus the word *American,* as in *Swedish American* or *Mexican American.* Capitalize the initial letters of both words and do not use a hyphen unless you are using the term as an adjective. Currently *black* and *African American* are acceptable. Some people prefer *Native American* over *American Indian,* but both terms are used in edited American English. Use the name of the specific American Indian group if you are writing about specific people. *Inuit* is currently the term preferred over *Eskimo.*

Be inclusive about people with disabilities

The *Publication Manual of the American Psychological Association* (5th ed.) offers some good advice: "Put people first, not their disability" (75). Write *people who are deaf* instead of *the deaf* and *a student who is quadriplegic* instead of *a quadriplegic student.* Avoid naming someone as a victim; *a person with cancer* is better than *a cancer victim. Disability* is the term preferred over *handicap.* The word *handicap* derives from *hand-in-cap,* a term referring to begging that carries negative connotations.

Be inclusive about people of different ages

Avoid bias by choosing accurate terms to describe age. If possible, use the person's age. *Eighty-two-year-old Adele Schumacher* is better than *elderly Adele Schumacher.*

Grammar

CHAPTER 22

Fragments, Run-ons, and Comma Splices

The most common sources of sentence errors are fragments, run-ons, and comma splices.

22a FRAGMENTS

Fragments are incomplete sentences. They are punctuated to look like sentences, but they lack a key element—often a subject or a verb—or else are a subordinate clause or phrase. Consider an example of a full sentence followed by a fragment:

> The university's enrollment rose unexpectedly during the fall semester. **Because the percentage of students who accepted offers of admission was much higher than previous years and fewer students than usual dropped out or transferred.**

When a sentence starts with *because,* we expect to find a main clause later. Instead, the *because* clause refers back to the previous sentence. The writer no doubt knew that the fragment gave reasons why enrollment rose, but a reader must stop to determine the connection.

In formal writing you should avoid fragments. Readers expect words punctuated as a sentence to be a complete sentence. They expect writers to complete their thoughts rather than force readers to guess the missing element.

Basic strategies for turning fragments into sentences

Incorporate the fragment into an adjoining sentence. In many cases you can incorporate the fragment into an adjoining sentence.

I was hooked on the ~~game. Playing~~ *game, playing* day and night.

Add the missing element. If you cannot incorporate a fragment into another sentence, add the missing element.

When aiming for the highest returns, ~~and~~ *investors* also ~~thinking~~ *should think* about the possible losses.

COMMON ERRORS

Recognizing fragments

If you can spot fragments, you can fix them. Grammar checkers can find some of them, but they miss many fragments and also identify other sentences wrongly as fragments. Ask these questions when you are checking for sentence fragments.

- **Does the sentence have a subject?** Except for commands, sentences need subjects:

  Jane spent every cent of credit she had available. **And then applied for more cards.**

- **Does the sentence have a complete verb?** Sentences require complete verbs. Verbs that end in *-ing* must have an auxiliary verb to be complete.

  Ralph keeps changing majors. **He trying to figure out what he really wants to do after college.**

- **If the sentence begins with a subordinate clause, is there a main clause in the same sentence?**

  Even though Seattle is cloudy much of the year, no American city is more beautiful when the sun shines. **Which is one reason people continue to move there.**

Remember:
1. A sentence must have a subject and complete verb.
2. A subordinate clause cannot stand alone as a sentence.

22b RUN-ON SENTENCES

While fragments are incomplete sentences, run-ons jam together two or more sentences, failing to separate them with appropriate punctuation.

Fixing run-on sentences

Take three steps to fix run-on sentences: (1) identify the problem, (2) determine where the run-on sentence needs to be divided, and (3) choose the punctuation that indicates the relationship between the main clauses.

COMMON ERRORS

Recognizing run-on sentences

When you read this sentence, you realize something is wrong.

> **I do not recall what kind of printer it was all I remember is that it could sort, staple, and print a packet at the same time.**

The problem is that the two main clauses are not separated by punctuation. The reader must look carefully to determine where one main clause stops and the next one begins.

> I do not recall what kind of printer it was **|** all I remember is that it could sort, staple, and print a packet at the same time.

A period should be placed after *was,* and the next sentence should begin with a capital letter:

> I do not recall what kind of printer it wa**s. A**ll I remember is that it could sort, staple, and print a packet at the same time.

Run-on sentences are major errors.

Remember: Two main clauses must be separated by correct punctuation.

---

1. Identify the problem. When you read your writing aloud, run-on sentences will often trip you up, just as they confuse readers. You can also search for subject and verb pairs to check for run-ons. If you find two main clauses with no punctuation separating them, you have a run-on sentence.

┌────SUBJ────┐ ┌────VERB────┐
Internet businesses are not **bound** to specific locations or old ways
┌S┐ ┌V┐
of running a business **they are** more flexible in allowing employees to
telecommute and to determine the hours they work.

2. Determine where the run-on sentence needs to be divided.

Internet businesses are not bound to specific locations or old ways of running a business | they are more flexible in allowing employees to telecommute and to determine the hours they work.

3. Determine the relationship between the main clauses. You will revise a run-on more effectively if you first determine the relationship between the main clauses and understand the effect or point you are trying to make. There are several punctuation strategies for fixing run-ons.

- **Insert a period.** This is the simplest way to fix a run-on sentence.

  Internet businesses are not bound to specific locations or old ways of running a business. They are more flexible in allowing employees to telecommute and to determine the hours they work.

  However, if you want to indicate the relationship between the two main clauses more clearly, you may want to choose one of the following strategies.

- **Insert a semicolon (and possibly a transitional word indicating the relationship between the two main clauses).**

  Internet businesses are not bound to specific locations or old ways of running a business; **therefore,** they are more flexible in allowing employees to telecommute and to determine the hours they work.

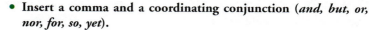

- **Insert a comma and a coordinating conjunction (*and, but, or, nor, for, so, yet*).**

  Internet businesses are not bound to specific locations or old ways of running a business, **so** they are more flexible in allowing employees to telecommute and to determine the hours they work.

- **Make one of the clauses subordinate.**

  Because Internet businesses are not bound to specific locations or old ways of running a business, they are more flexible in allowing employees to telecommute and to determine the hours they work.

22c COMMA SPLICES

Comma splices occur when two or more sentences are incorrectly joined by a comma: A comma links two clauses that could stand on their own. In this example, the comma following "classes" should be a period.

> Most of us were taking the same classes, if someone had a question, we would all help out.

Such sentences include a punctuation mark—a comma—separating two main clauses. However, a comma is not a strong enough punctuation mark to separate two main clauses.

Fixing comma splices

You have several options for fixing comma splices. Select the one that best fits where the sentence is located and the effect you are trying to achieve.

1. Change the comma to a period. Most comma splices can be fixed by changing the comma to a period.

It didn't matter that I worked in a windowless room for 40 hours a week. On
~~week, on~~ the Web I was exploring and learning more about distant people and places than I ever had before.

COMMON ERRORS

Recognizing comma splices

When you edit your writing, look carefully at sentences that contain commas. Does the sentence contain two main clauses? If so, are the main clauses joined by a comma and coordinating conjunction (*and, but, for, or, not, so, yet*)?

INCORRECT The ┌SUBJ┐**concept** of "nature" ┌VERB┐**depends** on the concept of human "culture," the ┌SUBJ┐ ┌V┐**problem is** that "culture" is itself shaped by "nature." [Two main clauses joined by only a comma]

CORRECT Even though the concept of "nature" depends on the concept of human "culture," "culture" is itself shaped by "nature." [Subordinate clause plus a main clause]

CORRECT The concept of "nature" depends on the concept of human "culture," but "culture" is itself shaped by "nature." [Two main clauses joined by a comma and coordinating conjunction]

The word *however* produces some of the most common comma splice errors. *However* usually functions to begin a main clause, and it should be punctuated with a semicolon rather than a comma.

INCORRECT The White House press secretary repeatedly vowed the Administration was not choosing a side between the two countries embroiled in conflict**, however** the developing foreign policy suggested otherwise.

CORRECT The White House press secretary repeatedly vowed the Administration was not choosing a side between the two countries embroiled in conflict**; however,** the developing foreign policy suggested otherwise. [Two main clauses joined by a semicolon]

Remember: Do not use a comma as a period.

2. Change the comma to a semicolon.   A semicolon indicates the close connection between the two main clauses.

> It didn't matter that I worked in a windowless room for 40 hours a *week;* ~~week,~~ on the Web I was exploring and learning more about distant people and places than I ever had before.

3. Insert a coordinating conjunction.   Other comma splices can be repaired by inserting a coordinating conjunction (*and, but, or, nor, so, yet, for*) to indicate the relationship of the two main clauses. The coordinating conjunction must be preceded by a comma.

> Digital technologies have intensified a global culture that affects us daily in large and small ways**, yet** their impact remains poorly understood.

4. Make one of the main clauses a subordinate clause.   If a comma splice includes one main clause that is subordinate to the other, rewrite the sentence using a subordinating conjunction.

> *Because community* ~~Community~~ is the vision of a great society trimmed down to the size of a small town, it is a powerful metaphor for real estate developers who sell a mini-utopia along with a house or condo.

5. Make one of the main clauses a phrase.   You can also rewrite one of the main clauses as a phrase.

> Community—**the vision of a great society trimmed down to the size of a small town**—is a powerful metaphor for real estate developers who sell a mini-utopia along with a house or condo.

C H A P T E R   2 3

Subject-Verb Agreement

A verb must match its subject. If the subject is singular (*I, you, he, she,* or *it*), the verb must take a singular form. If the subject is plural (*we, you, they*), the verb must take a plural form. Therefore, verbs are said to *agree in number* with their subjects. This single rule determines subject-verb agreement.

23a AGREEMENT IN THE PRESENT TENSE

When your verb is in the present tense, agreement in number is straightforward: The subject takes the base form of the verb in all but the third person singular. For example, the verb *walk,* in the present tense, agrees in number with most subjects in its base form:

FIRST PERSON SINGULAR	I walk
SECOND PERSON SINGULAR	You walk
FIRST PERSON PLURAL	We walk
SECOND PERSON PLURAL	You walk
THIRD PERSON PLURAL	They walk

Third person singular subjects are the exception to this rule. When your subject is in the third person singular (*he, it, Fido, Lucy, Mr. Jones*) you need to add an *s* or *es* to the base form of the verb.

THIRD PERSON SINGULAR (ADD *S*)	He walks. It walks. Fido walks.
THIRD PERSON SINGULAR (ADD *ES*)	Lucy goes. Mr. Jones goes.

23b SINGULAR AND PLURAL SUBJECTS

Follow these rules when you have trouble determining whether to use a singular or plural verb form.

Subjects joined by *and*

When two subjects are joined by *and,* treat them as a compound (plural) subject.

The teacher and the lawyer **are** headed west to start a commune.

Some compound subjects are treated as singular. These kinds of compounds generally work together as a single noun. Although they appear to be compound and therefore plural, these subjects take the singular form of the verb:

Rock and roll **remains** the devil's music, even in the twenty-first century.

When two nouns linked by *and* are modified by *every* or *each,* these two nouns are likewise treated as one singular subject:

Each night and day **brings** no new news of you.

An exception to this rule arises when the word *each* follows a compound subject. In these cases, usage varies depending on the number of the direct object.

The army and the navy each **have** their own air forces.

The owl and the pussycat each **has** a personal claim to fame.

Subjects joined by *or, either . . . or,* or *neither . . . nor*

If a subject is joined by *or, either . . . or,* or *neither . . . nor,* make sure the verb agrees with the subject closest to the verb.

┌─ SING ─┐ ┌─────── PLURAL ───────┐ ┌ PL ┐
Is it **the sky or the mountains** that **are** blue?

┌────── PLURAL ──────┐ ┌─ SING ─┐ ┌─ SING ─┐
Is it **the mountains or the sky** that **surrounds** us?

┌────── PLURAL ──────┐ ┌────── SING ──────┐ ┌ SING ┐
Neither the animals nor the zookeeper knows how to relock the gate.

┌─ SING ─┐ ┌────── PLURAL ──────┐ ┌ PL ┐
Either a coyote or several dogs were howling last night.

Subjects along with another noun

Verbs agree with the subject of a sentence, even when a subject is linked to another noun with a phrase like *as well as, along with,* or *alongside.*

These modifying phrases are usually set off from the main subject with commas.

———————— IGNORE THIS PHRASE ————————
Chicken, alongside various steamed vegetables, **is** my favorite meal.

— IGNORE THIS PHRASE —
Besides B. B. King, **John Lee Hooker and Muddy Waters** **are** my favorite blues artists of all time.

COMMON ERRORS

Subjects separated from verbs

The most common agreement errors occur when words come between the subject and verb. These intervening words do not affect subject-verb agreement. To ensure that you use the correct verb form, identify the subject and the verb. Ignore any phrases that come between them.

——————— IGNORE THIS PHRASE ———————
INCORRECT   **Students** at inner-city Washington High **reads** more than suburban students.

CORRECT   **Students** at inner-city Washington High **read** more than suburban students.

Students is plural and *read* is plural; subject and verb agree.

INCORRECT   **The whale shark**, the largest of all sharks, **feed** on plankton.

CORRECT   **The whale shark**, the largest of all sharks, **feeds** on plankton.

The plural noun *sharks* that appears between the subject *the whale shark* and the verb *feeds* does not change the number of the subject. The subject is singular and the verb is singular. Subject and verb agree.

Remember: When you check for subject-verb agreement, identify the subject and the verb. Ignore any words that come between them.

23c INDEFINITE PRONOUNS AS SUBJECTS

The choice of a singular or plural pronoun is determined by the **antecedent**—the noun that pronoun refers to. Indefinite pronouns, such as *some, few, all, someone, everyone,* and *each,* often do not refer to identifiable subjects; hence they have no antecedents. Most indefinite pronouns are singular and agree with the singular forms of verbs. Some, like *both* and *many,* are always plural and agree with the plural forms of verbs. Other indefinite pronouns are variable and can agree with either singular or plural verb forms, depending on the context of the sentence.

COMMON ERRORS

Agreement errors using *each*

The indefinite pronoun *each* is a frequent source of subject-verb agreement errors. If a pronoun is singular, its verb must be singular. This rule holds true even when the subject is modified by a phrase that includes a plural noun.

A common stumbling block to this rule is the pronoun *each. Each* is always treated as a singular pronoun in college writing. When *each* stands alone, the choice is easy to make:

INCORRECT	**Each are an outstanding student.**
CORRECT	**Each is an outstanding student.**

But when *each* is modified by a phrase that includes a plural noun, the choice of a singular verb form becomes less obvious:

INCORRECT	**Each of the girls are fit.**
CORRECT	**Each of the girls is fit.**
INCORRECT	**Each of our dogs get a present.**
CORRECT	**Each of our dogs gets a present.**

Remember: *Each* is always singular.

23d   COLLECTIVE NOUNS AS SUBJECTS

Collective nouns refer to groups (*audience, class, committee, crowd, family, government, group, jury, public, team*). When members of a group are considered as a unit, use singular verbs and singular pronouns.

> The **crowd is** unusually quiet at the moment, but **it** will get noisy soon.

When members of a group are considered as individuals, use plural verbs and plural pronouns.

> The **faculty have their** differing opinions on how to address the problems caused by reduced state support.

Sometimes collective nouns can be singular in one context and plural in another. Writers must decide which verb form to use based on sentence context.

> The **number** of people who live downtown **is** increasing.

> A **number** of people **are** moving downtown from the suburbs.

23e   INVERTED WORD ORDER

In English a sentence's subject usually comes before the verb: *The nights are tender*. Sometimes, however, you will come across a sentence with inverted word order: *Tender are the nights*. Here the subject of the sentence, *nights*, comes after the verb, *are*. Writers use inverted word order most often in forming questions. The statement *Cats are friendly* becomes a question when you invert the subject and the verb: *Are cats friendly?* Writers also use inverted word order for added emphasis or for style considerations.

Do not be confused by inverted word order. Locate the subject of your sentence, then make sure your verb agrees with that subject.

23f   AMOUNTS, NUMBERS, AND PAIRS

Subjects that describe amounts of money, time, distance, or measurement are singular and require singular verbs.

> **Three days is** never long enough to unwind.

Some subjects, such as courses of study, academic specializations, illnesses, and even some nations, are treated as singular subjects even though their names end in *-s* or *-es*. For example, *economics, news, ethics, measles,* and *the United States* all end in *-s* but are all singular subjects.

Economics is a rich field of study.

Other subjects require a plural verb form even though they refer to single items such as *jeans, slacks, glasses, scissors,* and *tweezers.* These items are all pairs.

My **glasses are** scratched.

 C H A P T E R   2 4

Verbs

As a reader you've had the experience of stumbling over a sentence, reading it three or four times before it makes sense. Often the cause of the confusion is a verb problem. Problems with verbs, fortunately, are easy to spot and fix if you know what to look for.

24a BASIC VERB FORMS

Almost all verbs in English have five possible forms. The exception is the verb *be*. Regular verbs follow this basic pattern:

Base form	Third person singular	Past tense	Past participle	Present participle
jump	jumps	jumped	jumped	jumping
like	likes	liked	liked	liking
talk	talks	talked	talked	talking
wish	wishes	wished	wished	wishing

Base form

The base form of the verb is the one you find listed in the dictionary. This form indicates an action or condition in the present.

I **like** New York in June.

Third person singular

Third person singular subjects include *he, she, it,* and the nouns they replace, as well as other pronouns, including *someone, anybody,* and *everything.* Present tense verbs in the third person singular end with an *s* or an *es.*

Ms. Nessan **speaks** in riddles.

Past tense

The past tense describes an action or condition that occurred in the past. For most verbs, the past tense is formed by adding *d* or *ed* to the base form of the verb.

She **inhaled** the night air.

Many verbs, however, have irregular past tense forms. (See Section 24b.)

Past participle

The past participle is used with *have* to form verbs in the perfect tense, with *be* to form verbs in the passive voice (see Section 18a), and to form adjectives derived from verbs.

PAST PERFECT	They **had gone** to the grocery store prematurely.
PASSIVE	The book **was written** thirty years before it **was published**.
ADJECTIVE	In the eighties, **teased** hair was all the rage.

COMMON ERRORS

Missing verb endings

Verb endings are not always pronounced in speech, especially in some dialects of English. It's also easy to omit these endings when you are writing quickly. Spelling checkers will not mark these errors, so you have to find them while proofreading.

INCORRECT	Jeremy **feel** as if he's catching a cold.
CORRECT	Jeremy **feels** as if he's catching a cold.
INCORRECT	Sheila **hope** she would get the day off.
CORRECT	Sheila **hoped** she would get the day off.

Remember: Check verbs carefully for missing _s_ or _es_ endings in the present tense and missing _d_ or _ed_ endings in the past tense.

Present participle

The present participle functions in one of three ways. Used with an auxiliary verb, it can describe a continuing action. The present participle can also function as a noun, known as a **gerund**, or as an adjective. The present participle is formed by adding _ing_ to the base form of a verb.

PRESENT PARTICIPLE	Wild elks **are competing** for limited food resources.
GERUND	**Sailing** around the Cape of Good Hope is rumored to bring good luck.
ADJECTIVE	We looked for shells in the **ebbing** tide.

24b IRREGULAR VERBS

A verb is **regular** when its past and past participle forms are created by adding _ed_ or _d_ to the base form. If this rule does not apply, the verb is

considered an **irregular** verb. Here are selected common irregular verbs and their basic conjugations.

Common irregular verbs

Base form	Past tense	Past participle
be (is, am, are)	was, were	been
become	became	become
bring	brought	brought
come	came	come
do	did	done
get	got	got or gotten
go	went	gone
have	had	had
know	knew	known
see	saw	seen

COMMON ERRORS

Confusing the past tense and past participle forms of irregular verbs

The past tense and past participle forms of irregular verbs are often confused. The most frequent error is using a past tense form instead of the past participle with *had*.

	PAST TENSE
INCORRECT	She had never **rode** a horse before.
	PAST PARTICIPLE
CORRECT	She had never **ridden** a horse before.
	PAST TENSE
INCORRECT	He had **saw** many alligators in Louisiana.
	PAST PARTICIPLE
CORRECT	He had **seen** many alligators in Louisiana.

Remember: Change any past tense verbs preceded by *had* to past participles.

24c TRANSITIVE AND INTRANSITIVE VERBS

Lay/lie, set/sit, and raise/rise

Do your house keys lay or lie on the kitchen table? Does a book set or sit on the shelf? *Raise/rise, lay/lie,* and *set/sit* are transitive and intransitive verbs that writers frequently confuse. Transitive verbs take direct objects— nouns that receive the action of the verb. Intransitive verbs act in sentences that lack direct objects.

> **TRANSITIVE** Henry **sets** the book [direct object, the book being set] on the shelf.
>
> **INTRANSITIVE** Henry **sits** down to read the book.

The following charts list the trickiest pairs of transitive and intransitive verbs and the correct forms for each verb tense. Pay special attention to *lay* and *lie,* which are irregular.

	lay (put something down)	**lie (recline)**
Present	lay, lays	lie, lies
Present participle	laying	lying
Past	laid	lay
Past participle	laid	lain

> **TRANSITIVE** Once you complete your test, please **lay** your pencil [direct object, the thing being laid down] on the desk.
>
> **INTRANSITIVE** The *Titanic* **lies** upright in two pieces at a depth of 13,000 feet.

	raise (elevate something)	**rise (get up)**
Present	raise, raises	rise, rises
Present participle	raising	rising
Past	raised	rose
Past participle	raised	risen

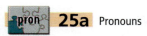

| | TRANSITIVE | We **raise** our glasses [direct object, the things being raised] to toast Uncle Han. |

TRANSITIVE   We **raise** our glasses [direct object, the things being raised] to toast Uncle Han.

INTRANSITIVE   The sun **rises** over the bay.

	set (place something)	sit (take a seat)
Present	set, sets	sit, sits
Present participle	setting	sitting
Past	set	sat
Past participle	set	sat

TRANSITIVE   Every morning Stanley **sets** two dollars [direct object, the things being set] on the table to tip the waiter.

INTRANSITIVE   I **sit** in the front seat if it's available.

CHAPTER 25

Pronouns

Pronouns are little words like *he, she, it, we, our, who,* and *mine* that stand for nouns and other pronouns. They are among the most frequently used words in English, but they also are a frequent source of problems in writing.

25a   PRONOUN CASE

Subject pronouns function as the subjects of sentences. **Object pronouns** function as direct or indirect objects. **Possessive pronouns** indicate ownership.

Subject pronouns	Object pronouns	Possessive pronouns
I	me	my, mine
we	us	our, ours

Subject pronouns	Object pronouns	Possessive pronouns
you	you	your, yours
he	him	his
she	her	her, hers
it	it	its
they	them	their, theirs
who	whom	whose

Pronouns in compound phrases

Picking the right pronoun sometimes can be confusing when the pronoun appears in a compound phrase.

> If we work together, you and **me** can get the job done quickly.

> If we work together, you and **I** can get the job done quickly.

Which is correct—*me* or *I*? Removing the other pronoun usually makes the choice clear.

> **INCORRECT** **Me** can get the job done quickly.

> **CORRECT** **I** can get the job done quickly.

We and *us* before nouns

Another pair of pronouns that can cause difficulty is *we* and *us* before nouns.

> **Us** friends must stick together.

> **We** friends must stick together.

Which is correct—*us* or *we*? Removing the noun indicates the correct choice.

> **INCORRECT** **Us** must stick together.

> **CORRECT** **We** must stick together.

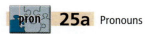 **25a** Pronouns

Who versus *whom*

Choosing between *who* and *whom* is often difficult, even for experienced writers. The distinction between *who* and *whom* is disappearing from spoken language. *Who* is more often used in spoken language, even when *whom* is correct.

COMMON ERRORS

Who or *Whom*

In writing, the distinction between *who* and *whom* is still often observed. *Who* and *whom* follow the same rules as other pronouns: *Who* is the subject pronoun; *whom* is the object pronoun. If you are dealing with an object, *whom* is the correct choice.

INCORRECT	**Who** did you send the letter to? **Who** did you give the present to?
CORRECT	To **whom** did you send the letter? **Whom** did you give the present to?

Who is always the right choice for the subject pronoun.

CORRECT	**Who** gave you the present? **Who** brought the cookies?

If you are uncertain of which one to use, try substituting *she* and *her* or *he* and *him*.

INCORRECT	You sent the letter to **she** [who]?
CORRECT	You sent the letter to **her** [whom]?
INCORRECT	**Him [Whom]** gave you the present?
CORRECT	**He [Who]** gave you the present?

Remember: *Who* = subject
**   *Whom* = object**

Whoever versus whomever

With the rule regarding *who* and *whom* in mind, you can distinguish between *whoever* and *whomever*. Which is correct?

> Her warmth touched **whoever** she met.

> Her warmth touched **whomever** she met.

In this sentence the pronoun functions as a direct object: Her warmth touched everyone she met, not someone touched her. Thus *whomever* is the correct choice.

Pronouns in comparisons

When you write a sentence using a comparison that includes *than* or *as* followed by a pronoun, usually you will have to think about which pronoun is correct. Which of the following is correct?

> Vimala is a faster swimmer than **him**.

> Vimala is a faster swimmer than **he**.

The test that will give you the correct answer is to add the verb that finishes the sentence—in this case, *is*.

| INCORRECT | Vimala is a faster swimmer than **him is**. |
| CORRECT | Vimala is a faster swimmer than **he is**. |

Adding the verb makes the correct choice evident.

Possessive pronouns

Possessive pronouns at times are confusing because possessive nouns are formed with apostrophes but possessive pronouns do not require apostrophes. Pronouns that use apostrophes are always **contractions**.

It's = It is
Who's = Who is
They're = They are

The test for whether to use an apostrophe is to determine whether the pronoun is possessive or a contraction. The most confusing pair is *its* and *it's*.

INCORRECT	**Its** a sure thing she will be elected. [Contraction]
CORRECT	**It's** a sure thing she will be elected. [**It is** a sure thing.]
INCORRECT	The dog lost **it's** collar. [Possessive]
CORRECT	The dog lost **its** collar.

Possessive pronouns before *-ing* verbs

Pronouns that modify an *-ing* verb (called a *gerund*) or an *-ing* verb phrase (*gerund phrase*) should appear in the possessive.

| INCORRECT | The odds of **you** making the team are excellent. |
| CORRECT | The odds of **your** making the team are excellent. |

25b PRONOUN AGREEMENT

Because pronouns usually replace or refer to other nouns, they must match those nouns in number and gender. The noun that the pronoun replaces is called its **antecedent**. If pronoun and antecedent match, they are in **agreement**. When a pronoun is close to the antecedent, usually there is no problem.

Maria forgot **her** coat.

The band **members** collected **their** uniforms.

Pronoun agreement errors often happen when pronouns and the nouns they replace are separated by several words.

INCORRECT

The **players**, exhausted from the double-overtime game, picked up **his** sweats and walked toward the locker rooms.

CORRECT

The **players**, exhausted from the double-overtime game, picked up **their** sweats and walked toward the locker rooms.

Careful writers make sure that pronouns match their antecedents.

Collective nouns

Collective nouns (such as *audience, class, committee, crowd, family, herd, jury, team*) can be singular or plural depending on whether the emphasis is on the group or on the particular individuals.

> CORRECT   The **committee** was unanimous in **its** decision.

> CORRECT   The **committee** put **their** opinions ahead of the goals of the unit.

COMMON ERRORS

Indefinite pronouns

Indefinite pronouns (such as *anybody, anything, each, either, everybody, everything, neither, none, somebody, something*) refer to unspecified people or things. Most take singular pronouns.

> INCORRECT   **Everybody** can choose **their** roommates.

> CORRECT   **Everybody** can choose **his or her** roommate.

> CORRECT   **All students** can choose **their** roommates.
> ALTERNATIVE

A few indefinite pronouns (*all, any, either, more, most, neither, none, some*) can take either singular or plural pronouns.

> CORRECT   **Some** of the shipment was damaged when **it** became overheated.

> CORRECT   **All** thought **they** should have a good seat at the concert.

A few pronouns are always plural (*few, many, several*).

> CORRECT   **Several** want refunds.

Remember: Words that begin with *any, some,* and *every* are usually singular.

COMMON ERRORS

Pronoun agreement with compound antecedents

Antecedents joined by *and* take plural pronouns.

CORRECT   **Moncef and Driss** practiced **their** music.

Exception: When compound antecedents are preceded by *each* or *every,* use a singular pronoun.

CORRECT   **Every male cardinal and warbler** arrives before the female to define **its** territory.

When compound antecedents are connected by *or* or *nor,* the pronoun agrees with the antecedent closer to it.

INCORRECT   **Either the Ross twins or Angela** should bring **their** CDs.

CORRECT   **Either the Ross twins or Angela** should bring **her** CDs.

BETTER   **Either Angela or the Ross twins** should bring **their** CDs.

When you put the plural *twins* last, the correct choice becomes the plural pronoun *their.*

Remember:
1. **Use plural pronouns for antecedents joined by *and*.**
2. **Use singular pronouns for antecedents preceded by *each* or *every*.**
3. **Use a pronoun that agrees with the nearest antecedent when compound antecedents are joined by *or* or *nor*.**

25c **AVOID SEXIST PRONOUNS**

English does not have a neutral singular pronoun for a group of mixed genders or a person of unknown gender. Referring to a group of mixed genders using male pronouns is unacceptable to many people. Unless the school in the following example is all male, many readers would object to the use of *his.*

SEXIST   **Each student** must select **his** courses using the online registration system.

One strategy is to use *her or his* or *his or her* instead of *his.*

CORRECT   **Each student** must select **his or her** courses using the online registration system.

Often you can avoid using *his or her* by changing the noun to the plural form.

BETTER   **All students** must select **their** courses using the online registration system.

In some cases, however, using *his or her* is necessary.

25d VAGUE REFERENCE

Pronouns can sometimes refer to more than one noun, thus confusing readers.

The **coach** rushed past the injured **player** to yell at the **referee**. **She** was hit in the face by a stray elbow.

You have to guess which person *she* refers to—the coach, the player, or the referee. Sometimes you cannot even guess the antecedent of a pronoun.

The new subdivision destroyed the last remaining habitat for wildlife within the city limits. **They** have ruined our city with their unchecked greed.

Whom does *they* refer to? the mayor and city council? the developers? the people who live in the subdivision? or all of the above?

Pronouns should never leave the reader guessing about antecedents. If different nouns can be confused as the antecedent, then the ambiguity should be clarified.

VAGUE   Mafalda's pet boa constrictor crawled across Tonya's foot. **She** was mortified.

BETTER   When Mafalda's pet boa constrictor crawled across Tonya's foot, **Mafalda** was mortified.

COMMON ERRORS

Vague use of *this*

Always use a noun immediately after *this, that, these, those,* and *some.*

VAGUE   Enrique asked Meg to remove the viruses on his computer. **This** was a bad idea.

Was it a bad idea for Enrique to ask Meg because she was insulted? Because she didn't know how? Because removing viruses would destroy some of Enrique's files?

BETTER   Enrique asked Meg to remove the viruses on his computer. **This imposition** on Meg's time made her resentful.

Remember: Ask yourself "*this* what?" and add the noun that *this* refers to.

CHAPTER 26

Shifts

Unintentional shifts in tense, mood, voice, or number often distract readers. Watch for these types of shifts and edit them out of your writing unless you are certain that their purpose is clear and evident to your readers.

26a   SHIFTS IN TENSE

Appropriate shifts in verb tense

Changes in verb tense are sometimes necessary to indicate a shift in time.

PAST
TO FUTURE

Because Oda **won** the lottery [PAST TENSE], she **will quit** [FUTURE TENSE] her job at the hospital as soon as her supervisor **finds** [PRESENT TENSE] a qualified replacement.

COMMON ERRORS

Unnecessary tense shift

Notice the tense shift in the following example.

INCORRECT
In May of 2000 the "I Love You" virus **crippled** [PAST TENSE] the computer systems of major American companies and **irritated** [PAST TENSE] millions of private computer users. As the virus **generates** [PRESENT TENSE] millions of emails and **erases** [PRESENT TENSE] millions of computer files, companies such as Ford and Time Warner **are forced** [PRESENT TENSE] to shut down their clogged email systems.

The second sentence shifts unnecessarily to the present tense, confusing the reader. Did the "I Love You" virus have its heyday several years ago, or is it still wreaking havoc now? Changing the verbs in the second sentence to the past tense eliminates the confusion.

CORRECT
In May of 2000 the "I Love You" virus **crippled** [PAST TENSE] the computer systems of major American companies and **irritated** [PAST TENSE] millions of private computer users. As the virus **generated** [PAST TENSE] millions of emails and **erased** [PAST TENSE] millions of computer files, companies such as Ford and Time Warner **were forced** [PAST TENSE] to shut down their clogged email systems.

Remember: Shift verb tense only when you are referring to different time periods.

Inappropriate shifts in verb tense

Be careful to avoid confusing your reader with unnecessary shifts in verb tense.

INCORRECT
While Brazil **looks** [PRESENT TENSE] to ecotourism to fund rain forest preservation, other South American nations **relied** [PAST TENSE] on foreign aid and conservation efforts.

The shift from present tense (*looks*) to past tense (*relied*) is confusing. Correct the mistake by putting both verbs in the present tense.

Correct	PRES TENSE While Brazil **looks** to ecotourism to fund rain forest PRES TENSE preservation, other South American nations **rely** on for- eign aid and conservation efforts.

26b SHIFTS IN MOOD

Verbs can be categorized into three moods—indicative, imperative, and subjunctive—defined by the functions they serve.

Indicative verbs state facts, opinions, and questions.

Fact	NASA **plans** to return the Space Shuttle to flight this year.

Imperative verbs make commands, give advice, and make requests.

Command	**Investigate** the cause of the accident so the Shuttle can return to flight.

Subjunctive verbs express wishes, unlikely or untrue situations, hypothetical situations, requests with *that* clauses, and suggestions.

Unlikely or untrue situation	If fixing the Shuttle **were** as simple as the news media made it out to be, NASA would be flying missions by now.

Be careful not to shift from one mood to another in mid-sentence.

Incorrect	If the government **were** to shift funding priorities away from the Shuttle, NASA scientists **lose** even more time in getting the Shuttle flying again.

The sudden shift from subjunctive to indicative mood in this sentence is confusing. Are the scientists losing time now, or is losing time a likely result of a government funding shift? Revise the sentence to keep both verbs in the subjunctive.

Correct	If the government **were** to shift funding priorities away from the Shuttle, NASA scientists **would lose** even more time in getting the Shuttle flying again.

26c SHIFTS IN VOICE

Watch for unintended shifts from active (*I ate the cookies*) to passive voice (*the cookies were eaten*).

> **INCORRECT** The sudden storm **toppled** several trees and numerous windows **were shattered**.

The unexpected shift from active voice (*toppled*) to passive (*were broken*) forces readers to wonder whether it was the sudden storm, or something else, that broke the windows.

> **CORRECT** The sudden storm **toppled** several trees and **shattered** numerous windows.

Revising the sentence to eliminate the shift to passive voice (see Section 18a) also improves its parallel structure (see 20c).

26d SHIFTS IN PERSON AND NUMBER

Sudden shifts from third person (*he, she, it, one*) to first (*I, we*) or second (*you*) are confusing to readers and often indicate a writer's uncertainty about how to address a reader. We often make such shifts in spoken English, but in formal writing shifts in person need to be recognized and corrected.

> **INCORRECT** When **one** is reading a magazine, **you** often see several different type fonts used on a single page.

The shift from third person to second person in this sentence is confusing.

> **CORRECT** When reading a magazine **you** often see several different type fonts used on a single page.

Similarly, shifts from singular to plural subjects (see Section 23b) within a single sentence also confuse readers. See the examples on the next page. The revised sentence eliminates a distracting and unnecessary shift from plural to singular.

> **INCORRECT** Administrators often make more money than **professors**, but only **a professor** has frequent contact with students.

> **CORRECT** Administrators often make more money than **professors**, but only **professors** have frequent contact with students.

C H A P T E R 2 7
Modifiers

Modifiers come in two varieties: adjectives and adverbs. The same words can function as adjectives or adverbs, depending on what they modify.

Adjectives modify

nouns—*iced* tea, *power* forward
pronouns—He is *brash*.

Adverbs modify

verbs—*barely* reach, drive *carefully*
adjectives—*truly* brave activist, *shockingly* red lipstick
other adverbs—*not* soon forget, *very* well
clauses—*Honestly,* I find ballet boring.

Adjectives answer the questions *Which one? How many?* and *What kind?* Adverbs answer the questions *How often? To what extent? When? Where? How?* and *Why?*

27a CHOOSE THE CORRECT MODIFIER

Use the correct forms of comparatives and superlatives

Comparative modifiers weigh one thing against another. They either end in *er* or are preceded by *more*.

Road bikes are **faster** on pavement than mountain bikes.

The **more courageous** juggler tossed flaming torches.

Superlative modifiers compare three or more items. They either end in *est* or are preceded by *most*.

April is the **hottest** month in New Delhi.

Wounded animals are the **most ferocious**.

When should you add a suffix instead of *more* or *most*? The following guidelines work in most cases:

Adjectives

- For adjectives of one or two syllables, add *er* or *est*.

  redder, heaviest

- For adjectives of three or more syllables, use *more* or *most*.

  more viable, most powerful

Adverbs

- For adverbs of one syllable, use *er* or *est*.

  nearer, slowest

- For adverbs with two or more syllables, use *more* or *most*.

  more convincingly, most humbly

Some frequently used comparatives and superlatives are irregular. The following list can help you become familiar with them.

Adjective	Comparative	Superlative
good	better	best
bad	worse	worst
little (amount)	less	least
many, much	more	most
Adverb	**Comparative**	**Superlative**
well	better	best
badly	worse	worst

Do not use both a suffix (*er* or *est*) and *more* or *most*.

INCORRECT	The service at Jane's Restaurant is **more slower** than the service at Alphonso's.
CORRECT	The service at Jane's Restaurant is **slower** than the service at Alphonso's.

Be sure to name the elements being compared if they are not clear from the context.

UNCLEAR COMPARATIVE	Mice are **cuter**.
CLEAR	Mice are **cuter than rats**.
UNCLEAR SUPERLATIVE	Nutria are the **creepiest**.
CLEAR	Nutria are the **creepiest rodents**.

Absolute modifiers are words that represent an unvarying condition and thus aren't subject to the degrees that comparative and superlative constructions convey. Common absolute modifiers include *complete, ultimate,* and *unique. Unique,* for example, means "one of a kind." There's nothing else like it. Thus something cannot be *very unique* or *totally unique.* It is either unique or it isn't. Absolute modifiers should not be modified by comparatives (*more* + modifier or modifier + *er*) or superlatives (*most* + modifier or modifier + *est*).

Double negatives

In English, as in mathematics, two negatives equal a positive. Avoid using two negative words in one sentence, or you'll end up saying the opposite of what you mean. The following are negative words that you should avoid doubling up:

barely	nobody	nothing
hardly	none	scarcely
neither	no one	

INCORRECT, DOUBLE NEGATIVE	**Barely no one** noticed that the pop star lip-synched during the whole performance.

CORRECT, **SINGLE NEGATIVE**	**Barely anyone** noticed that the pop star lip-synched during the whole performance.
INCORRECT, **DOUBLE NEGATIVE**	When the pastor asked if anyone had objections to the marriage, **nobody** said **nothing.**
CORRECT, **SINGLE NEGATIVE**	When the pastor asked if anyone had objections to the marriage, **nobody** said **anything**.

27b PLACE ADJECTIVES CAREFULLY

As a general rule, the closer you place a modifier to the word it modifies, the less the chance you will confuse your reader.

Place adjective phrases and clauses carefully

Adjective phrases or clauses can be confusing if they are separated from the word they modify.

CONFUSING	**Watching from the ground below**, the kettle of broadwing hawks circled high above the observers.

Is the kettle of hawks watching from the ground below? You can fix the problem by putting the modified subject immediately after the modifier or placing the modifier next to the modified subject.

BETTER	The kettle of broadwing hawks circled high above the **observers who were watching from the ground below**.
BETTER	**Watching from the ground below**, the **observers** saw a kettle of broadwing hawks circle high above them.

Place one-word adjectives before the modified word(s)

One-word adjectives almost always precede the word or words they modify.

Pass the **hot** sauce, please.

When one-word adjectives are not next to the word or words being modified, they can create misunderstandings.

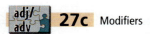

> **UNCLEAR** Before his owner withdrew him from competition, the **fiercest rodeo's bull** injured three riders.

Readers may think *fiercest* modifies *rodeo's* instead of *bull*. Placing the adjective before *bull* will clarify the meaning.

> **BETTER** Before his owner withdrew him from competition, the **rodeo's fiercest bull** injured three riders.

27c PLACE ADVERBS CAREFULLY

For the most part, the guidelines for adverb placement are not as complex as the guidelines for adjective placement.

Place adverbs before or after the words they modify

Single-word adverbs and adverbial clauses and phrases can usually sit comfortably either before or after the words they modify.

> Dimitri **quietly** **walked** down the hall.
>
> Dimitri **walked** **quietly** down the hall.

Conjunctive adverbs—*also, however, instead, likewise, then, therefore, thus,* and others—are adverbs that show how ideas relate to one another. They prepare a reader for contrasts, exceptions, additions, conclusions, and other shifts in an argument. Conjunctive adverbs can usually fit well into more than one place in the sentence. In the following example, *however* could fit in three different places.

BETWEEN TWO MAIN CLAUSES

Professional football players earn exorbitant salaries; **however**, they pay for their wealth with lifetimes of chronic pain and debilitating injuries.

WITHIN SECOND MAIN CLAUSE

Professional football players earn exorbitant salaries; they pay for their wealth, **however**, with lifetimes of chronic pain and debilitating injuries.

AT END OF SECOND MAIN CLAUSE

Professional football players earn exorbitant salaries; they pay for their wealth with lifetimes of chronic pain and debilitating injuries **however**.

Subordinating conjunctions—words such as *after, although, because, if, since, than, that, though, when,* and *where*—often begin **adverb clauses**. Notice that we can place adverb clauses with subordinating conjunctions either before or after the word(s) being modified:

After someone in the audience yelled, he **forgot** the lyrics.

He **forgot** the lyrics **after someone in the audience yelled**.

COMMON ERRORS

Placement of limiting modifiers

Words such as *almost, even, hardly, just, merely, nearly, not, only,* and *simply* are called limiting modifiers. Although people often play fast and loose with their placement in everyday speech, limiting modifiers should always go immediately before the word or words they modify in your writing. Many writers have difficulty with the placement of *only*. Like other limiting modifiers, *only* should be placed immediately before the word it modifies.

INCORRECT	The Gross Domestic Product **only** gives one indicator of economic growth.
CORRECT	The Gross Domestic Product gives **only** one indicator of economic growth.

The word *only* modifies *one* in this sentence, not *Gross Domestic Product*.

Remember: Place limiting modifiers immediately before the word(s) they modify.

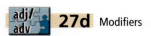

27d HYPHENS WITH COMPOUND MODIFIERS

When to hyphenate

Hyphenate a compound modifier that precedes a noun.

When a compound modifier precedes a noun, you should usually hyphenate the modifier. A **compound modifier** consists of words that join together as a unit to modify a noun. Since the first word modifies the second, compound modifiers will not make sense if the word order is reversed.

middle-class values   self-fulfilling prophecy

best-selling novel   tough-minded friend

well-known musician   ill-mannered child

Hyphenate a phrase when it is used as a modifier that precedes a noun.

out-of-body experience   step-by-step instructions

all-you-can-eat buffet   all-or-nothing payoff

devil-may-care attitude   over-the-counter drug

Hyphenate the prefixes *pro-, anti-, post-, pre-, neo-*, and *mid-* before proper nouns.

pro-Catholic sentiment   mid-Atlantic states

neo-Nazi racism   anti-NAFTA protests

pre-Columbian art   post-Freudian theory

Hyphenate a compound modifier with a number when it precedes a noun.

eighteenth-century drama   one-way street

tenth-grade class   47-minute swim

When not to hyphenate

Do not hyphenate a compound modifier that follows a noun.

The instructor's approach is student centered.

Among country music fans Lyle Lovett is well known.

Do not hyphenate compound modifiers when the first word is *very* or ends in *ly*.

newly recorded data   very cold day

freshly painted bench   very jolly baby

27e REVISE DANGLING MODIFIERS

Some modifiers are ambiguous because they could apply to more than one word or clause. Dangling modifiers are ambiguous for the opposite reason; they don't have a word to modify. In such cases the modifier is usually an introductory clause or phrase. What is being modified should immediately follow the phrase, but in the following sentence it is absent.

After bowling a perfect game, Surfside Lanes hung Marco's photo on the wall.

Neither the subject of the sentence, *Surfside Lanes,* nor the direct object, *Marco's photo,* is capable of bowling a perfect game. Since a missing noun or pronoun causes a dangling modifier, simply rearranging the sentence will not resolve the problem.

You can eliminate a dangling modifier in two ways:

1. Insert the noun or pronoun being modified immediately after the introductory modifying phrase.

   After bowling a perfect game, **Marco** was honored by having his photo hung on the wall at Surfside Lanes.

2. Rewrite the introductory phrase as an introductory clause to include the noun or pronoun.

   After **Marco** bowled a perfect game, Surfside Lanes hung his photo on the wall.

COMMON ERRORS

Dangling modifiers

A dangling modifier does not seem to modify anything in a sentence; it dangles, unconnected to the word or words it presumably is intended to modify. Frequently, it produces some funny results:

> **When still a girl**, my father joined the army.

It sounds like *father* was once a girl. The problem is that the subject, *I*, is missing:

> **When I was still a girl**, my father joined the army.

Dangling modifiers usually occur at the head of a sentence when a subject is implied but never stated.

INCORRECT After lifting the heavy piano up the stairs, the apartment door was too small to get it through.

CORRECT After lifting the heavy piano up the stairs, **we discovered** the apartment door was too small to get it through.

Whenever you use a modifier, ask yourself whether its relationship to the word it modifies will be clear to your reader. What is clear to you may not be clear to your audience. Writing, like speaking, is an exercise in making your own thoughts explicit.

Remember: Modifiers should be clearly connected to the words they modify, especially at the beginning of sentences.

CHAPTER 28

Grammar for Nonnative Speakers

Many writers say that the main challenges of writing in a second language are grammar and vocabulary. While grammar and vocabulary are important, sometimes too much focus on the details of writing can take your attention away from other issues that affect your ability to communicate effectively. If you have learned to write in a language other than English, you may have noticed some differences between writing in English and in your native language. Readers of business correspondence in English, for example, expect communication to be direct, concise, and explicit, and often become impatient with the indirect style of address sometimes preferred in business writing in other languages.

When you write in an unfamiliar situation, it may be helpful to find a few examples of the type of writing you are trying to produce. If you are writing a cover letter to accompany a résumé, for example, ask your friends to share similar cover letters with you and look for the similarities in the ways they present themselves in writing in that situation. Ask them to read their letters out loud, and to explain the decisions they made as they wrote and revised their letters. Talk with them about how and why they wrote their cover letters, and you will develop a better understanding of the ways writers in English respond to a given writing situation than you may be able to get from simply studying the format of a cover letter in a textbook.

28a NOUNS

Perhaps the most troublesome conventions for nonnative speakers are those that guide usage of the common articles *the, a,* and *an.* To understand how articles work in English, you must first understand how the language uses **nouns**.

Kinds of nouns

There are two basic kinds of nouns. A **proper noun** begins with a capital letter and names a unique person, place, or thing: *George W. Bush, Russia, Eiffel Tower*. In the following list, note that each word refers to someone or something so specific that it bears a name.

Proper nouns

Beethoven	Michael Jordan	South Korea
Concorde	New York Yankees	Africa
Empire State Building	Picasso	Stockholm
Honda	Queen Elizabeth	Lake Michigan
Thanksgiving	Virginia Woolf	New Hampshire

The other basic kind of noun is called a **common noun**. Common nouns do not name a unique person, place, or thing: *man, country, tower*.

Count and noncount nouns

Common nouns can be classified as either *count* or *noncount*. **Count nouns** can be made plural, usually by adding *-s* (*finger, fingers*) or by using their plural forms (*person, people; datum, data*). **Noncount nouns** cannot be counted directly and cannot take the plural form (*information,* but not *informations; garbage,* but not *garbages*). Some nouns can be either count or noncount, depending on how they are used. *Hair* can refer to either a strand of hair, where it serves as a count noun, or a mass of hair, where it becomes a noncount noun.

28b ARTICLES

Articles indicate that a noun is about to appear, and they clarify what the noun refers to. There are only two kinds of articles in English, definite and indefinite:

1. **the:** *The* is a **definite article**, meaning that it refers to (1) a specific object already known to the reader, (2) one about to be made known to the reader, or (3) a unique object.

COMMON ESL ERRORS

Singular and plural forms of count nouns

Count nouns are simpler to quantify than noncount nouns. But remember that English requires you to state both singular and plural forms of nouns consistently and explicitly. Look at the following sentences.

INCORRECT	The three **bicyclist** shaved their **leg** before the big race.
CORRECT	The three **bicyclists** shaved their **legs** before the big race.

In the first sentence, readers would understand that the plural form of *bicyclist* is implied by the quantifier *three* and that the plural form of *leg* is implied by the fact that bicyclists have two legs. (If they don't, you would hope that the writer would have made that clear already!) Nevertheless, correct form in English is to indicate the singular or plural nature of a count noun explicitly, in every instance.

Remember: English requires you to use plural forms of count nouns even if a plural number is otherwise indicated.

2. **a, an:** The **indefinite articles** *a* and *an* refer to an object whose specific identity is not known to the reader. The only difference between *a* and *an* is that *a* is used before a consonant sound (*man, friend, yellow*), while *an* is used before a vowel sound (*animal, enemy, orange*).

Look at these sentences, identical except for their articles, and imagine that each is taken from a different newspaper story:

Rescue workers lifted **the** man to safety.

Rescue workers lifted **a** man to safety.

By use of the definite article *the,* the first sentence indicates that the reader already knows something about the identity of this man and his needing to be rescued. The news story has already referred to him. The sentence also suggests that this was the only man rescued, at least in this particular part of the story.

The indefinite article *a* in the second sentence indicates that the reader does not know anything about this man. Either this is the first time the news story has referred to him, or there are other men in need of rescue. When deciding whether to use the definite or indefinite article, ask yourself whether the noun refers to something specific or unique, or whether it refers to something general. *The* is used for specific or unique nouns; *a* and *an* are used for nonspecific or general nouns.

COMMON ESL ERRORS

Articles with count and noncount nouns

Knowing how to distinguish between count and noncount nouns can help you decide which article to use. Noncount nouns are never used with the indefinite articles *a* or *an*.

INCORRECT   Maria jumped into **a** water.

CORRECT   Maria jumped into **the** water.

No articles are used with noncount and plural count nouns when you wish to state something that has a general application.

INCORRECT   **The** water is a precious natural resource.

CORRECT   Water is a precious natural resource.

INCORRECT   **The** soccer players tend to be quick and agile.

CORRECT   Soccer players tend to be quick and agile.

Remember:

1. **Noncount nouns are never used with *a* and *an*.**
2. **Noncount and plural nouns used to make general statements do not take articles.**

28c VERBS

The verb system in English can be divided between simple verbs like *run, speak,* and *look,* and verb phrases like *may have run, have spoken,* and *will be looking.* In these examples, the words that appear before the main verbs—*may, have, will,* and *be*—are called **auxiliary verbs** (also called **helping verbs**). Helping verbs, as their name suggests, exist to help express something about the action of main verbs: for example, when the action occurs (tense), whether the subject acted or was acted upon (voice), or whether or not an action occurred.

Indicating tense and voice with *be* verbs

Like the other auxiliary verbs *have* and *do, be* changes form to signal tense. In addition to *be* itself, the **be verbs** are *is, am, are, was, were,* and *been.* To show ongoing action, *be* verbs are followed by the present participle, which is a verb with an *-ing* ending:

INCORRECT	I **am think** of all the things I'd rather **be do**.
CORRECT	I **am thinking** of all the things I'd rather **be doing**.
INCORRECT	He **was run** as fast as he could.
CORRECT	He **was running** as fast as he could.

To show that an action is being done to, rather than by, the subject, follow *be* verbs with the past participle (a verb usually ending in *-ed, -en,* or *-t*):

INCORRECT	The movie **was direct** by John Woo.
CORRECT	The movie **was directed** by John Woo.
INCORRECT	The complaint **will be file** by the victim.
CORRECT	The complaint **will be filed** by the victim.

Modal auxiliary verbs

Modal auxiliary verbs *will, would, can, could, may, might, shall, must,* and *should* express conditions like possibility, permission, speculation, expectation, obligation, and necessity. Unlike the auxiliary verbs *be, have,* and *do,* modal verbs do not change form based on the grammatical subject of the sentence (*I, you, she, he, it, we, they*).

Two basic rules apply to all uses of modal verbs. First, modal verbs are always followed by the simple form of the verb. The simple form is the verb by itself, in the present tense, such as *have* but not *had, having,* or *to have.*

INCORRECT	She should **studies** harder to pass the exam.
CORRECT	She should **study** harder to pass the exam.

The second rule is that you should not use modals consecutively.

INCORRECT	If you work harder at writing, you **might could** improve.
CORRECT	If you work harder at writing, you **might** improve.

Ten conditions that modals express

- **Speculation:** If you had flown, you **would** have arrived yesterday.
- **Ability:** She **can** run faster than Jennifer.
- **Necessity:** You **must** know what you want to do.
- **Intention:** He **will** wash his own clothes.
- **Permission:** You **may** leave now.
- **Advice:** You **should** wash behind your ears.
- **Possibility:** It **might** be possible to go home early.
- **Assumption:** You **must** have stayed up late last night.
- **Expectation:** You **should** enjoy the movie.
- **Order:** You **must** leave the building.

PART SIX

Punctuation
and Mechanics

29 COMMAS

a Commas with introductory elements
b Commas with compound clauses
c Commas with nonrestrictive modifiers
d Commas with items in a series
e Commas with coordinate adjectives
f Commas with quotations
g Commas with dates, numbers, titles, and addresses
h Commas to avoid confusion
i Unnecessary commas

30 SEMICOLONS AND COLONS

a Semicolons with closely related main clauses
b Semicolons together with commas
c Colons in sentences
d Colons with lists

31 DASHES AND PARENTHESES

a Dashes and parentheses to set off information
b Dashes and parentheses versus commas
c Other punctuation with parentheses

32 APOSTROPHES

a Possessives
b Contractions and omitted letters
c Plurals of letters, symbols, and words referred to as words

33 QUOTATION MARKS

a Direct quotations
b Titles of short works
c Other uses of quotation marks
d Other punctuation with quotation marks

34 OTHER PUNCTUATION MARKS

a Periods   d. Brackets
b Question marks   e. Ellipses
c Exclamation points   f. Slashes

35 CAPITALIZATION, ITALICS, ABBREVIATIONS, NUMBERS

a Capital letters   d. Acronyms
b Italics   e. Numbers
c Abbreviations

C H A P T E R   2 9

Commas

Commas give readers vital clues about how to read a sentence. They tell readers when to pause and indicate how the writer's ideas relate to one another.

29a COMMAS WITH INTRODUCTORY ELEMENTS

Introductory elements like conjunctive adverbs and introductory phrases usually need to be set off by commas. Introductory words or phrases signal a shift in ideas or a particular arrangement of ideas; they help direct the reader's attention to the writer's most important points. Commas force the reader to pause and take notice of these pivotal elements.

When a conjunctive adverb or introductory phrase begins a sentence, the comma follows.

> **Therefore,** the suspect could not have been at the scene of the crime.

> **Above all,** remember to let water drip from the faucets if the temperature drops below freezing.

When a conjunctive adverb comes in the middle of a sentence, set it off with commas preceding and following.

> If you really want to prevent your pipes from freezing, **however,** you should insulate them before the winter comes.

Occasionally the conjunctive adverb or phrase blends into a sentence so smoothly that a pause would sound awkward.

> **AWKWARD**   Even if you take every precaution, the pipes in your home may freeze, **nevertheless.**

> **BETTER**   Even if you take every precaution, the pipes in your home may freeze **nevertheless.**

COMMON ERRORS

Commas with long introductory modifiers

Long subordinate clauses or phrases that begin sentences should be followed by a comma. The following sentence lacks the needed comma.

INCORRECT   Because cell phones now have organizers and email Palm Pilots may soon become another technology of the past.

When you read this sentence, you likely had to go back to sort it out. The words *organizers and email Palm Pilots* tend to run together. When the comma is added, the sentence is easier to understand because the reader knows where the subordinate clause ends and where the main clause begins:

CORRECT   Because cell phones now have organizers and email, Palm Pilots may soon become another technology of the past.

How long is a long introductory modifier? Short introductory adverbial phrases and clauses of five words or fewer can get by without the comma if the omission does not mislead the reader. Using the comma is still correct after short introductory adverbial phrases and clauses:

CORRECT   In the long run stocks have always done better than bonds.

CORRECT   In the long run, stocks have always done better than bonds.

Remember: Put commas after long introductory modifiers.

29b   COMMAS WITH COMPOUND CLAUSES

Two main clauses joined by a coordinating conjunction (*and, or, so, yet, but, nor, for*) form a compound sentence. Writers sometimes get confused about when to insert a comma before a coordinating conjunction.

COMMON ERRORS

Identifying compound sentences that require commas

The easiest way to distinguish between compound sentences and sentences with phrases that follow the main clause is to isolate the part that comes after the conjunction. If the part that follows the conjunction can stand on its own as a complete sentence, insert a comma. If it cannot, omit the comma.

MAIN CLAUSE PLUS PHRASES

Mario thinks he lost his passport while riding the bus or by absentmindedly leaving it on the counter when he checked into the hostel.

Look at what comes after the coordinating conjunction *or:*

by absentmindedly leaving it on the counter when he checked into the hostel

This group of words is not a main clause and cannot stand on its own as a complete sentence. Do not set it off with a comma.

MAIN CLAUSES JOINED WITH A CONJUNCTION

On Saturday Mario went to the American consulate to get a new passport, but the officer told him that replacement passports could not be issued on weekends.

Read the clause after the coordinating conjunction *but:*

the officer told him that replacement passports could not be issued on weekends

This group of words can stand on its own as a complete sentence. Thus, it is a main clause; place a comma before *but.*

Remember:

1. Place a comma before the coordinating conjunction (*and, but, for, or, nor, so, yet*) if there are two main clauses.

2. Do not use a comma before the coordinating conjunction if there is only one main clause.

Use a comma to separate main clauses

Main clauses carry enough grammatical weight to be punctuated as sentences. When two main clauses are joined by a coordinating conjunction, place a comma before the coordinating conjunction in order to distinguish them.

> Sandy borrowed two boxes full of records on Tuesday**, and** she returned them on Friday.

Very short main clauses joined by a coordinating conjunction do not need commas.

> She called **and** she called, but no one answered.

Do not use a comma to separate two verbs with the same subject

> **INCORRECT**   Sandy borrowed two boxes full of records on Tuesday**, and** returned them on Friday.

Sandy is the subject of both *borrowed* and *returned*. This sentence has only one main clause; it should not be punctuated as a compound sentence.

> **CORRECT**   Sandy borrowed two boxes full of records on Tuesday **and** returned them on Friday.

Do not use a comma to separate a main clause from a restrictive clause or phrase

When clauses and phrases that follow the main clause are essential to the meaning of a sentence, they should not be set off with a comma.

> **INCORRECT**   Sandy plans to borrow Felicia's record collection**,** while Felicia is on vacation.
>
> **CORRECT**   Sandy plans to borrow Felicia's record collection while Felicia is on vacation.

COMMON ERRORS

Do not use a comma to set off a *because* clause that follows a main clause

Writers frequently place unnecessary commas before *because* and similar subordinate conjunctions that follow a main clause. *Because* is not a coordinating conjunction; thus it should not be set off by a comma unless the comma improves readability.

INCORRECT   I struggled to complete my term papers last year, because I didn't know how to type.

CORRECT   I struggled to complete my term papers last year because I didn't know how to type.

But do use a comma after an introductory *because* clause.

INCORRECT   Because Danny left his red jersey at home Coach Russell benched him.

CORRECT   Because Danny left his red jersey at home, Coach Russell benched him.

Remember: Use a comma after a *because* clause that begins a sentence. Do not use a comma to set off a *because* clause that follows a main clause.

29c COMMAS WITH NONRESTRICTIVE MODIFIERS

Imagine that you are sending a friend a group photo that includes your aunt. Which sentence is correct?

In the back row the woman wearing the pink hat is my aunt.

In the back row the woman, wearing the pink hat, is my aunt.

Both sentences can be correct depending on what is in the photo. If there are three women standing in the back row and only one is wearing a pink hat, this piece of information is necessary for identifying your aunt. In this case the sentence without commas is correct because it identifies your aunt as the woman wearing the pink hat. Such necessary modifiers are **restrictive** and do not require commas.

If only one woman is standing in the back row, *wearing the pink hat* is extra information and not necessary to identify your aunt. The modifier in this case is **nonrestrictive** and is set off by commas.

Distinguish restrictive and nonrestrictive modifiers

You can distinguish restrictive and nonrestrictive modifiers by deleting the modifier and then deciding whether the remaining sentence is changed. For example, delete the modifier *still stained by its bloody Tianamen Square crackdown* from the following sentence:

> Some members of the Olympic Site Selection Committee wanted to prevent China**,** **still stained by its bloody Tianamen Square crack-down,** from hosting the 2008 games.

The result leaves the meaning of the main clause unchanged.

> Some members of the Olympic Site Selection Committee wanted to prevent China from hosting the 2008 games.

The modifier is nonrestrictive and should be set off by commas.

Pay special attention to appositives

Clauses and phrases can be restrictive or nonrestrictive, depending on the context. Often the difference is obvious, but some modifiers require close consideration, especially appositives. An **appositive** is a noun or noun phrase that identifies or adds information to the noun preceding it.

Consider the following pair.

1 The best-selling vehicles SUVs usually rate the lowest on fuel efficiency.

2 The best-selling vehicles, SUVs, usually rate the lowest on fuel efficiency.

Which is correct? The appositive *SUVs* is not essential to the meaning of the sentence and offers additional information. Thus, it is a nonrestrictive appositive and should be set off with commas. Sentence 2 is correct.

Use commas to mark off parenthetical expressions

A **parenthetical expression** provides information or commentary that usually is not essential to the sentence's meaning.

INCORRECT   My mother much to my surprise didn't say anything when she saw my pierced nose.

CORRECT   My mother, much to my surprise, didn't say anything when she saw my pierced nose.

29d COMMAS WITH ITEMS IN A SERIES

In a series of three or more items, place a comma after each item except the last one. The comma between the last two items goes before the coordinating conjunction (*and, or, nor, but, so, for, yet*).

Health officials in Trenton, Manhattan, and the Bronx have all reported new cases of the West Nile virus.

29e COMMAS WITH COORDINATE ADJECTIVES

Coordinate adjectives are two or more adjectives that each modify the same noun independently. Coordinate adjectives that are not linked by *and* must be separated by a comma.

After the NASDAQ bubble burst in 2000 and 2001, the Internet technology companies that remained were no longer the **fresh-faced, giddy** kids of Wall Street.

You can recognize coordinate adjectives by reversing their order; if their meaning remains the same, the adjectives are coordinate and must be linked by *and* or separated by a comma.

Commas are not used between **cumulative adjectives**. Cumulative adjectives are two or more adjectives that work together to modify a noun: *deep blue sea, inexpensive mountain bike*. If reversing their order changes the description of the noun (or violates the order of English, such as *mountain inexpensive bike*), the adjectives are cumulative and should not be separated by a comma.

The following example doesn't require a comma in the cumulative adjective series *massive Corinthian*.

> Visitors to Rome's Pantheon pass between the **massive Corinthian** columns flanking the front door.

We know they are cumulative because reversing their order to read *Corinthian massive* would alter the way they modify *columns*—in this case, so much so that they no longer make sense.

29f COMMAS WITH QUOTATIONS

Properly punctuating quotations with commas can be tricky unless you know a few rules about when and where to use commas.

When to use commas with quotations

Commas set off phrases that attribute quotations to a speaker or writer, such as *he argues, they said,* and *she writes.*

> "When you come to a fork in the road**,**" said Yogi Berra**,** "take it!"

If the attribution follows a quotation that is a complete sentence, replace the period that normally would come at the end of the quotation with a comma.

INCORRECT   "Simplicity of language is not only reputable but perhaps even sacred**.**" writes Kurt Vonnegut.

CORRECT   "Simplicity of language is not only reputable but perhaps even sacred**,**" writes Kurt Vonnegut.

When an attribution is placed in the middle of a quotation, put the comma preceding the attribution within the quotation mark just before the phrase.

When not to use commas with quotations

Do not replace a question mark or exclamation point with a comma.

INCORRECT "Who's on first**,**" Costello asked Abbott.

CORRECT "Who's on first**?**" Costello asked Abbott.

Not all phrases that mention the author's name are attributions. When quoting a term or using a quotation within a subordinate clause, do not set off the quotation with commas.

"Stonewall" Jackson gained his nickname at the First Battle of Bull Run when General Barnard Bee shouted to his men that Jackson was "standing like a stone wall."

29g COMMAS WITH DATES, NUMBERS, TITLES, AND ADDRESSES

Some of the easiest comma rules to remember are the ones we use every day in dates, numbers, personal titles, place names, direct address, and brief interjections.

Commas with dates

Use commas to separate the day of the week from the month and to set off a year from the rest of the sentence.

Monday**,** November 18**,** 2002

On July 27**,** 2007**,** the opening ceremony of the World Scout Jamboree will be televised.

Do not use a comma when the month immediately precedes the year.

April 2008

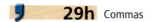

Commas with numbers

Commas mark off thousands, millions, billions, and so on.

> 16,500,000

> However, do not use commas in street addresses or page numbers.

> page 1542

> 7602 Elm Street

Commas with personal titles

When a title follows a person's name, set the title off with commas.

> Marcus Welby, MD

Commas with place names

Place a comma between street addresses, city names, state names, and countries.

> Write to the president at 1600 Pennsylvania Avenue, Washington, DC 20500.

Commas in direct address

When addressing someone directly, set off that person's name in commas.

> I was happy to get your letter yesterday, Jamie.

Commas with brief interjections

Use commas to set off brief interjections like *yes* and *no,* as well as short questions that fall at the ends of sentences.

> Have another piece of pie, won't you?

29h COMMAS TO AVOID CONFUSION

Certain sentences can confuse readers if you do not indicate where they should pause within the sentence. Use a comma to guide a reader through these usually compact constructions.

| UNCLEAR | With supplies low prices of gasoline and fuel oil will increase. |

This sentence could be read as meaning *With supplies, low prices will increase*.

| CLEAR | With supplies low, prices of gasoline and fuel oil will increase. |

29i UNNECESSARY COMMAS

Do not place a comma between a subject and the main verb.

| INCORRECT | American children of immigrant parents, often do not speak their parents' native language. |
| CORRECT | American children of immigrant parents often do not speak their parents' native language. |

However, you do use commas to set off modifying phrases that separate subjects from verbs.

| CORRECT | Steven Pinker, author of *The Language Instinct*, argues that the ability to speak and understand language is an evolutionary adaptive trait. |

Do not use a comma with a coordinating conjunction unless it joins two main clauses. (See the Common Errors box on page 219.)

INCORRECT	Susana thought finishing her first novel was hard, but soon learned that getting a publisher to buy it was much harder.
CORRECT	Susana thought finishing her first novel was hard but soon learned that getting a publisher to buy it was much harder.
CORRECT	Susana thought finishing her first novel was hard, but **she** soon learned that getting a publisher to buy it was much harder.

Do not use a comma after a subordinating conjunction such as *although, despite,* or *while*.

> **INCORRECT**   Although, soccer is gaining popularity in the States, it will never be as popular as football or baseball.

> **CORRECT**   Although soccer is gaining popularity in the States, it will never be as popular as football or baseball.

Some writers mistakenly use a comma with *than* to try to heighten the contrast in a comparison.

> **INCORRECT**   Any teacher will tell you that acquiring critical thinking skills is more important, than simply memorizing information.

> **CORRECT**   Any teacher will tell you that acquiring critical thinking skills is more important than simply memorizing information.

A common mistake is to place a comma after *such as* or *like* before introducing a list.

> **INCORRECT**   Many hourly workers, such as, waiters, dishwashers, and cashiers, do not receive health benefits from their employers.

> **CORRECT**   Many hourly workers, such as waiters, dishwashers, and cashiers, do not receive health benefits from their employers.

CHAPTER 30
Semicolons and Colons

Semicolons and colons are punctuation marks that link closely related ideas. They allow writers to emphasize the relationships between elements of a sentence, often using dramatic pauses to direct readers' attention to the most important ideas.

30a SEMICOLONS WITH CLOSELY RELATED MAIN CLAUSES

Why use semicolons? Sometimes we want to join two main clauses to form a complete sentence in order to indicate their close relationship. We can connect them with a comma and a coordinating conjunction like *or, but,* or *and.* To create variation in sentence style and avoid wordiness, you can omit the comma and coordinating conjunction, and insert a semicolon between the two clauses.

Semicolons can join only clauses that are grammatically equal. In other words, they join main clauses only to other main clauses, not to phrases or subordinate clauses. Look at the following examples:

INCORRECT
————— MAIN CLAUSE —————
Gloria's new weightlifting program will help her recover
————— PARTICIPIAL PHRASE —————
from knee surgery; doing a series of squats and presses
with a physical therapist.

CORRECT
————— MAIN CLAUSE —————
Gloria's new weightlifting program will help her recover
————— MAIN CLAUSE —————
from knee surgery; a physical therapist leads her through
a series of squats and presses.

Do not use a semicolon to introduce quotations

Use a comma or colon instead.

INCORRECT   Robert Frost's poem "Mending Wall" contains this line; "Good fences make good neighbors."

CORRECT   Robert Frost's poem "Mending Wall" contains this line: "Good fences make good neighbors."

Do not use a semicolon to introduce lists

INCORRECT   William Shakespeare wrote four romance plays at the end of his career; *The Tempest, The Winter's Tale, Cymbeline,* and *Pericles.*

CORRECT   William Shakespeare wrote four romance plays at the end of his career: *The Tempest, The Winter's Tale, Cymbeline,* and *Pericles.*

30b   SEMICOLONS TOGETHER WITH COMMAS

When an item in a series already includes a comma, adding more commas to separate it from the other items will only confuse the reader. Use semicolons instead of commas between items in a series that have internal punctuation.

> **CONFUSING**   The church's design competition drew entries from as far away as Gothenberg, Sweden, Caracas, Venezuela, and Athens, Greece.

> **CLEARER**   The church's design competition drew entries from as far away as Gothenberg, Sweden; Caracas, Venezuela; and Athens, Greece.

30c   COLONS IN SENTENCES

Like semicolons, colons can join two closely related main clauses (complete sentences). Colons indicate that what follows will explain or expand on what comes before the colon. Use a colon in cases where the second main clause interprets or sums up the first.

> Internet retailers have a limited customer base: Only those who have Internet access can become e-shoppers.

You may choose to capitalize the first word of the main clause following the colon or leave it lowercase. Either is correct as long as you are consistent throughout your text.

Colons linking main clauses with appositives

A colon calls attention to an appositive, a noun, or a noun phrase that renames the noun preceding it. If you're not certain whether a colon would be appropriate, put *namely* in its place. If *namely* makes sense when you read the main clause followed by the appositive, you probably need to insert a colon instead of a comma. Remember, the clause that precedes the colon must be a complete sentence.

> I know the perfect person for the job, **namely** me.

The sentence makes sense with *namely* placed before the appositive. Thus, a colon is appropriate.

> I know the perfect person for the job: me.

Never capitalize a word following a colon unless the word starts a complete sentence or is normally capitalized.

Colons joining main clauses with quotations

Use a colon to link a main clause and a quotation that interprets or sums up the clause. Be careful not to use a colon to link a phrase with a quotation.

INCORRECT: NOUN PHRASE–COLON–QUOTATION

> President Roosevelt's strategy to change the nation's panicky attitude during the Great Depression: "We have nothing to fear," he said, "but fear itself."

CORRECT: MAIN CLAUSE–COLON–QUOTATION

> President Roosevelt's strategy to end the Great Depression was to change the nation's panicky attitude: "We have nothing to fear," he said, "but fear itself."

The first example is incorrect because there is no main verb in the first part of the sentence and thus it is a phrase rather than a main clause. The second example adds the verb (*was*), making the first part of the sentence a main clause.

30d COLONS WITH LISTS

Use a colon to join a main clause to a list. The main clauses in these cases sometimes include the phrases *the following* or *as follows*. Remember that a colon cannot join a phrase or an incomplete clause to a list.

COMMON ERRORS

Colons misused with lists

Some writers think that anytime they introduce a list, they should insert a colon. Colons are used correctly only when a complete sentence precedes the colon.

INCORRECT　Jessica's entire wardrobe for her trip to Cancun included: two swimsuits, one pair of shorts, two T-shirts, a party dress, and a pair of sandals.

CORRECT　Jessica's entire wardrobe for her trip to Cancun included two swimsuits, one pair of shorts, two T-shirts, a party dress, and a pair of sandals.

CORRECT　Jessica jotted down what she would need for her trip: two swimsuits, one pair of shorts, two T-shirts, a party dress, and a pair of sandals.

Remember: A colon should be placed only after a clause that can stand by itself as a sentence.

INCORRECT: NOUN PHRASE—COLON—LIST

Three posters decorating Juan's apartment: an old Santana concert poster, a view of Mount Rainier, and a Diego Rivera mural.

CORRECT: MAIN CLAUSE—COLON—LIST

Juan bought three posters to decorate his apartment: an old Santana concert poster, a view of Mount Rainier, and a Diego Rivera mural.

CHAPTER 31

Dashes and Parentheses

Dashes and parentheses can be excellent tools for setting off and calling attention to information that comments on your ideas. They serve as visual cues to the reader of a sudden break in thought or change in sentence structure. Note that dashes (formed with two hyphens or the em-dash character in a word processor) and hyphens are not the same. **Hyphens** punctuate words; **dashes** punctuate sentences.

31a DASHES AND PARENTHESES TO SET OFF INFORMATION

Dashes and parentheses call attention to groups of words. In effect, they tell the reader that a group of words is not part of the main clause and should be given extra attention. If you want to make an element stand out, especially in the middle of a sentence, use parentheses or dashes instead of commas.

Dashes with final elements

A dash is often used to set off a phrase or subordinate clause at the end of a sentence to offer significant comments about the main clause. Dashes can also anticipate a shift in tone at the end of a sentence.

> A full-sized SUV can take you wherever you want to go in style—if your idea of style is a gas-guzzling tank.

Parentheses with additional information

Parentheses are more often used for identifying information, afterthoughts or asides, examples, and clarifications. You can place full sentences, fragments, or brief terms within parentheses.

> Some argue that SUVs (the best-selling vehicles on the market for three years running) are the primary cause of recent gas shortages.

DASHES AND PARENTHESES VERSUS COMMAS

Like commas, parentheses and dashes enclose material that adds, explains, or digresses. However, the three punctuation marks are not interchangeable. The mark you choose depends on how much emphasis you want to place on the material. Dashes indicate the most emphasis. Parentheses offer somewhat less, and commas offer less still.

COMMAS INDICATE A MODERATE LEVEL OF EMPHASIS

Bill covered the new tattoo on his bicep, a pouncing tiger, because he thought it might upset our mother.

COMMON ERRORS

Do not use dashes as periods

Do not use dashes to separate two main clauses (clauses that can stand as complete sentences). Use dashes to separate main clauses from subordinate clauses and phrases when you want to emphasize the subordinate clause or phrase.

INCORRECT: MAIN CLAUSE–DASH–MAIN CLAUSE

I was one of the few women in my computer science classes—most of the students majoring in computer science at that time were men.

CORRECT: MAIN CLAUSE–DASH–PHRASE

I was one of the few women in computer science—a field then dominated by men.

Remember: Dashes are not periods and should not be used as periods.

PARENTHESES LEND A GREATER LEVEL OF EMPHASIS

I'm afraid to go bungee jumping (though my brother tells me it's less frightening than a roller coaster).

DASHES INDICATE THE HIGHEST LEVEL OF EMPHASIS AND, SOMETIMES, SURPRISE AND DRAMA

Christina felt as though she had been punched in the gut; she could hardly believe the stranger at her door was really who he claimed to be—the brother she hadn't seen in twenty years.

31c OTHER PUNCTUATION WITH PARENTHESES

Parentheses around letters or numbers that order a series within a sentence make the list easier to read.

Angela Creider's recipe for becoming a great novelist is to (1) set aside an hour during the morning to write, (2) read what you've written out loud, (3) revise your prose, and (4) repeat every morning for the next thirty years.

Abbreviations made from the first letters of words are often used in place of the unwieldy names of institutions, departments, organizations, or terms. In order to show the reader what the abbreviation stands for, the first time it appears in a text the writer must state the complete name, followed by the abbreviation in parentheses.

The University of California, Santa Cruz (UCSC) supports its mascot, the banana slug, with pride and a sense of humor. And although it sounds strange to outsiders, UCSC students are even referred to as "the banana slugs."

COMMON ERRORS

Using periods, commas, colons, and semicolons with parentheses

When an entire sentence is enclosed in parentheses, place the period before the closing parenthesis.

INCORRECT   Our fear of sharks, heightened by movies like *Jaws*, is vastly out of proportion with the minor threat sharks actually pose. (Dying from a dog attack, in fact, is much more likely than dying from a shark attack).

CORRECT   Our fear of sharks, heightened by movies like *Jaws*, is vastly out of proportion with the minor threat sharks actually pose. (Dying from a dog attack, in fact, is much more likely than dying from a shark attack.)

When the material in parentheses is part of the sentence and the parentheses fall at the end of the sentence, place the period outside the closing parenthesis.

INCORRECT   Reports of sharks attacking people are rare (much rarer than dog attacks.)

CORRECT   Reports of sharks attacking people are rare (much rarer than dog attacks).

Place commas, colons, and semicolons after the closing parenthesis.

Remember: When an entire sentence is enclosed in parentheses, place the period inside the closing parenthesis; otherwise, put the punctuation outside the closing parenthesis.

C H A P T E R 3 2

Apostrophes

Apostrophes have three basic functions: to indicate possession, to mark contractions and omitted letters, and to form certain plurals.

32a POSSESSIVES

Nouns and indefinite pronouns (for example, *everyone, anyone*) that indicate possession or ownership are marked by attaching an apostrophe and an *-s* or an apostrophe only to the end of the word.

Singular nouns and indefinite pronouns

For singular nouns and indefinite pronouns, add an apostrophe plus *-s: -'s*. Even singular nouns that end in *-s* usually follow this principle.

Iris**'s** coat

everyone**'s** favorite

a woman**'s** choice

There are a few exceptions to adding *-'s* for singular nouns:

- **Awkward pronunciations** *Herodotus' travels, Jesus' sermons*
- **Official names of certain places, institutions, companies** *Governors Island, Teachers College of Columbia University, Mothers Café, Saks Fifth Avenue, Walgreens Pharmacy*. Note, however, that many companies do include the apostrophe: *Denny's Restaurant, Macy's, McDonald's, Wendy's Old Fashioned Hamburgers*.

Plural nouns

For plural nouns that do not end in *-s*, add an apostrophe plus *-s: -'s*.

media**'s** responsibility

children**'s** section

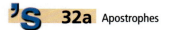 **32a** Apostrophes

For plural nouns that end in *-s*, add only an apostrophe at the end.

> attorneys' briefs
>
> the Kennedys' legacy

Compound nouns

For compound nouns, add an apostrophe plus *-s* to the last word of the compound noun: *-'s*.

> mayor of Cleveland's speech

Two or more nouns

For joint possession, add an apostrophe plus *-s* to the final noun: *-'s*.

> mother and dad's yard

When people possess or own things separately, add an apostrophe plus *-s* to each noun: *-'s*.

> Roberto's and Edward's views are totally opposed.

COMMON ERRORS

Possessive forms of personal pronouns never take the apostrophe

INCORRECT   *her's, it's, our's, your's, their's*

The bird sang in **it's** cage.

CORRECT   *hers, its, ours, yours, theirs*

The bird sang in **its** cage.

Remember: It's = It is

32b CONTRACTIONS AND OMITTED LETTERS

In speech we often leave out sounds and syllables of familiar words. These omissions are noted with apostrophes.

Contractions

Contractions combine two words into one, using the apostrophe to mark what is left out.

I am ⟶ I'm		we are ⟶ we're	
I would ⟶ I'd		they are ⟶ they're	
you are ⟶ you're		cannot ⟶ can't	
you will ⟶ you'll		do not ⟶ don't	
he is ⟶ he's		does not ⟶ doesn't	
she is ⟶ she's		will not ⟶ won't	
it is ⟶ it's			

Omissions

Using apostrophes to signal omitted letters is a way of approximating speech in writing. They can make your writing look informal and slangy, and overuse can become annoying in a hurry.

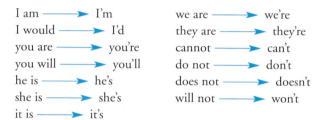

rock and roll ⟶ rock'n' roll
the 1960s ⟶ the '60s
neighborhood ⟶ 'hood

32c PLURALS OF LETTERS, SYMBOLS, AND WORDS REFERRED TO AS WORDS

When to use apostrophes to make plurals

The trend is away from using apostrophes to form plurals of letters, symbols, and words referred to as words. Most readers now prefer 1960s to the

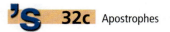
older form, 1960's. In a few cases adding the apostrophe and *s* is still used, as in this old saying:

Mind your p's and q's.

The apostrophe is still used when omitting it would cause confusion.

as   is   us

a's   i's   u's

Most readers would read the first row as words: "as," "is,"and "us." The writer intends to refer to the letters themselves, so the apostrophe is needed to distinguish "a's" (several letters) from "as" (a word). Words used as words are italicized and their plural formed by adding an *s* not in italics, instead of an apostrophe and *s*. Words in quotation marks, however, typically use apostrophe and *s*.

When not to use apostrophes to make plurals

Do not use an apostrophe to make family names plural.

INCORRECT   You've heard of keeping up with the Jones's.

CORRECT   You've heard of keeping up with the Joneses.

COMMON ERRORS

Do not use an apostrophe to make a noun plural

INCORRECT   The two government's agreed to meet.

CORRECT   The two governments agreed to meet.

INCORRECT   The video game console's of the past were one-dimensional.

CORRECT   The video game consoles of the past were one-dimensional.

Remember: Add only -s = plural
Add apostrophe plus -s = possessive

CHAPTER 33

Quotation Marks

Quotation marks set off quotations from surrounding text. But they also do other jobs that lend clarity to writing, like indicating certain kinds of titles, noting the novel use of a word, and showing that a word is being used as a word. Quotation marks are among the most commonly used and misused marks of punctuation.

33a DIRECT QUOTATIONS

Use quotation marks to enclose direct quotations

Enclose direct quotations—someone else's words repeated verbatim—in quotation marks.

> Anne Lamont advises writers to look at everything with compassion, even something as seemingly inconsequential as a chipmunk: "I don't want to sound too Cosmica Rama here, but in those moments, you see that you and the chipmunk are alike, are part of a whole" (98).

Do not use quotation marks with indirect quotations

Do not enclose an indirect quotation—a paraphrase of someone else's words—in quotation marks. However, do remember that you need to cite your source not only when you quote directly but also when you paraphrase or borrow ideas.

> Anne Lamont encourages writers to become compassionate observers who ultimately see themselves as equals to everything else, even something as seemingly inconsequential as a chipmunk (98).

Do not use quotation marks with block quotations

When a quotation is long enough to be set off as a block quotation, do not use quotation marks. MLA style defines long quotations as four or more lines of prose or poetry. APA style defines a long quotation as one of more than forty words.

In the following example, notice that the long quotation is indented and quotation marks are omitted. Also notice that the parenthetical citation in long quotations comes after the period.

> Complaints about maintenance in the dorms have been on the rise ever since the physical plant reorganized its crews into teams in August. One student's experience is typical:
>
>> When our ceiling started dripping, my roommate and I went to our resident director right away to file an emergency maintenance request. Apparently the physical plant felt that "emergency" meant they could get around to it in a week or two. By the fourth day without any word from a maintenance person, the ceiling tiles began to fall and puddles began to pool on our carpet. (Trillo)
>
> The physical plant could have avoided expensive ceiling tile and carpet repairs if it had responded to the student's request promptly.

33b   TITLES OF SHORT WORKS

While the titles of longer works such as books, magazines, and newspapers are italicized or underlined, titles of shorter works should be set off with quotation marks. Use quotation marks with the following kinds of titles:

SHORT STORIES	"Light Is Like Water," by Gabriel García Márquez
MAGAZINE ARTICLES	"Race against Death," by Erin West
NEWSPAPER ARTICLES	"Cincinnati Mayor Declares Emergency," by Liz Sidoti
SHORT POEMS	"We Real Cool," by Gwendolyn Brooks
ESSAYS	"Self-Reliance," by Ralph Waldo Emerson

The exception.   Don't put the title of your own paper in quotation marks. If the title of another short work appears within the title of your paper, retain the quotation marks around the short work.

33c OTHER USES OF QUOTATION MARKS

Quotation marks around a term can indicate that the writer is using the term in a novel way, often with skepticism, irony, or sarcasm. The quotation marks indicate that the writer is questioning the term's conventional definition.

Italics are usually used to indicate that a word is being used as a word, rather than standing for its conventional meaning. However, quotation marks are correct in these cases as well.

Beginning writers sometimes confuse "their," "they're," and "there."

COMMON ERRORS

Quotations within quotations

Single quotation marks are used to indicate a quotation within a quotation. In the following example single quotation marks clarify who is speaking. The rules for placing punctuation with single quotation marks are the same as the rules for placing punctuation with double quotation marks.

INCORRECT When he showed the report to Paul Probius, Michener reported that Probius "took vigorous exception to the sentence "He wanted to close down the university," insisting that we add the clarifying phrase "as it then existed"" (Michener 145).

CORRECT When he showed the report to Paul Probius, Michener reported that Probius "took vigorous exception to the sentence 'He wanted to close down the university,' insisting that we add the clarifying phrase 'as it then existed'" (Michener 145).

Remember: Single quotation marks are used for quotations within quotations.

33d OTHER PUNCTUATION WITH QUOTATION MARKS

The rules for placing punctuation with quotation marks fall into three general categories.

Periods and commas with quotation marks

Place periods and commas inside closing quotation marks.

> **INCORRECT** "The smartest people", Dr. Geisler pointed out, "tell themselves the most convincing rationalizations".
>
> **CORRECT** "The smartest people," Dr. Geisler pointed out, "tell themselves the most convincing rationalizations."

Colons and semicolons with quotation marks

Place colons and semicolons outside closing quotation marks.

> **INCORRECT** "From Stettin in the Baltic to Trieste in the Adriatic, an iron curtain has descended across the Continent;" Churchill's statement rang through Cold War politics for the next fifty years.
>
> **CORRECT** "From Stettin in the Baltic to Trieste in the Adriatic, an iron curtain has descended across the Continent"; Churchill's statement rang through Cold War politics for the next fifty years.

Exclamation points, question marks, and dashes with quotation marks

When an exclamation point, question mark, or dash belongs to the original quotation, place it inside the closing quotation mark. When it applies to the entire sentence, place it outside the closing quotation mark.

IN THE ORIGINAL QUOTATION

"Are we there yet?" came the whine from the back seat.

APPLIED TO THE ENTIRE SENTENCE

Did the driver in the front seat respond, "Not even close"?

CHAPTER 34

Other Punctuation Marks

Periods, question marks, and exclamation points indicate the conclusion of a sentence and tell the reader how to read it. Brackets, ellipses, and slashes occur much less often, but they also have important uses.

34a PERIODS

Periods at the ends of sentences

Place a period at the end of a complete sentence if it is not a direct question or an exclamatory statement. As the term suggests, a direct question asks a question outright. Indirect questions, on the other hand, report the asking of a question.

Periods with quotation marks and parentheses

When a quotation falls at the end of a sentence, place the period inside the closing quotation marks.

> Although he devoted decades to a wide range of artistic and political projects, Allen Ginsberg is best known as the author of the poem "Howl."

When a parenthetical phrase falls at the end of a sentence, place the period outside the closing parenthesis. When parentheses enclose a whole sentence, place the period inside the closing parenthesis.

Periods with abbreviations

Many abbreviations require periods; however, there are few set rules. Use the dictionary to check how to punctuate abbreviations on a case-by-case basis. The rules for punctuating two types of abbreviations do remain consistent: Postal abbreviations for states and most abbreviations for organizations do not require periods. When an abbreviation with a period falls at the end of a sentence, do not add a second period to conclude the sentence.

INCORRECT   Her flight arrives at 6:22 p.m..

CORRECT   Her flight arrives at 6:22 p.m.

Periods as decimal points

Decimal points are periods that separate integers from tenths, hundredths, and so on.

99.98% pure silver   98.6° Fahrenheit
on sale for $399.97   2.6 liter engine

Since large numbers with long strings of zeros can be difficult to read accurately, writers sometimes shorten them using decimal points. In this way, 16,600,000 can be written as 16.6 million.

34b   QUESTION MARKS

Question marks with direct questions

Place a question mark at the end of a direct question. A direct question is one that the questioner puts to someone outright. In contrast, an indirect question merely reports the asking of a question. Question marks give readers a cue to read the end of the sentence with rising inflection. Read the following sentences aloud. Hear how your inflection rises in the second sentence to convey the direct question.

INDIRECT QUESTION

Desirée asked whether Dan rides his motorcycle without a helmet.

DIRECT QUESTION

Desirée asked, "Does Dan ride his motorcycle without a helmet?"

Question marks with quotations

When a quotation falls at the end of a direct question, place the question mark outside the closing quotation mark.

Did Abraham Lincoln really call Harriet Beecher Stowe "the little lady who started this big war"?

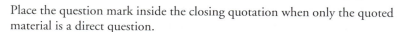
Place the question mark inside the closing quotation when only the quoted material is a direct question.

> Slowly scientists are beginning to answer the question, "Is cancer a genetic disease?"

When quoting a direct question in the middle of a sentence, place a question mark inside the closing quotation mark and place a period at the end of the sentence.

> Market researchers estimate that asking Burger World's customers "Do you want fries with that?" is responsible for a 15% boost in their french fries sales.

34c EXCLAMATION POINTS

Exclamation points to convey strong emotion

Exclamation points conclude sentences and, like question marks, tell the reader how a sentence should sound. They indicate strong emotion. Use exclamation points sparingly in formal writing; they are rarely appropriate in academic and professional prose.

Exclamation points with emphatic interjections

Exclamation points can convey a sense of urgency with brief interjections. Interjections can be incorporated into sentences or stand on their own.

> Run! They're about to close the doors to the jetway.

Exclamation points with quotation marks

In quotations, exclamation points follow the same rules as question marks. If a quotation falls at the end of an exclamatory statement, place the exclamation point outside the closing quotation mark.

> The singer forgot the words to "America the Beautiful"!

When quoting an exclamatory statement at the end of a sentence that is not itself exclamatory, place the exclamation point inside the closing quotation mark.

Jerry thought his car would be washed away in the flood, but Anna jumped into action, declaring, "Not if I can help it!"

34d BRACKETS

While brackets (sometimes called *square brackets*) look quite similar to parentheses, the two perform different functions. Brackets have a narrow set of uses.

Brackets to provide clarification within quotation marks

Use brackets if you are interjecting a comment of your own or clarifying information within a direct quotation. In the following example the writer quotes a sentence with the pronoun *they*, which refers to a noun in a previous, unquoted sentence. The material in brackets clarifies to whom the pronoun refers.

The Harris study found that "In the last three years, they [Gonzales Junior High students] averaged 15% higher on their mathematics assessment tests than their peers in Northridge County."

Brackets within parentheses

Since parentheses within parentheses might confuse readers, use brackets to enclose parenthetical information within a parenthetical phrase.

Representative Patel's most controversial legislation (including a version of the hate crimes bill [HR 99-108] the house rejected two years ago) has a slim chance of being enacted this session.

34e ELLIPSES

Ellipses let a reader know that a portion of a passage is missing. You can use ellipses to keep quotations concise and direct readers' attention to what is important to the point you are making. An ellipsis is a string of three periods with spaces separating the periods.

Ellipses to indicate an omission from a quotation

When you quote only a phrase or short clause from a sentence, you usually do not need to use ellipses.

> Mao Zedong first used "let a hundred flowers blossom" in a Beijing speech in 1957.

Except at the beginning of a quotation indicate omitted words with an ellipsis.

THE ORIGINAL SOURCE

"The female praying mantis, so named for the way it holds its front legs together as if in prayer, tears off her male partner's head during mating. Remarkably, the headless male will continue the act of mating. This brutal dance is a stark example of the innate evolutionary drive to pass genes onto offspring; the male praying mantis seems to live and die only for this moment."

AN ELLIPSIS INDICATES OMITTED WORDS

"The female praying mantis ... tears off her male partner's head during mating."

When the ellipsis is at the end of a sentence, place the period or question mark after the ellipsis and follow with the closing quotation mark.

WORDS OMITTED AT THE END OF A SENTENCE

"This brutal dance is a stark example of the innate evolutionary drive to pass genes onto offspring.... "

34f   SLASHES

Slashes to indicate alternative words

Slashes between two words indicate that a choice between them is to be made. When using slashes for this purpose, do not put a space between the slash and words.

> **INCORRECT** Maya was such an energetic baby that her exhausted parents wished she had come with an on **/** off switch.
>
> **CORRECT** Maya was such an energetic baby that her exhausted parents wished she had come with an on**/**off switch.

Slashes with fractions

Place a slash between the numerator and the denominator in a fraction. Do not put any spaces around the slash.

> **INCORRECT** 3 **/** 4
>
> **CORRECT** 3**/**4

C H A P T E R   3 5

Capitalization, Italics, Abbreviations, Numbers

Of course you know that you should capitalize the first word of a sentence, but you may not be as familiar with the other functions capital letters perform. Capital letters and italics also assist readers by indicating certain kinds and uses of words.

Abbreviations and acronyms are used much less often in writing for general audiences than in scientific and technical writing. The use of numbers also varies considerably from technical to general writing.

35a   CAPITAL LETTERS

Capitalize the initial letters of proper nouns (nouns that name particular people, places, and things). Capitalize the initial letters of proper adjectives (adjectives based on the names of people, places, and things).

African **A**merican bookstore   **A**vogadro's number   **I**rish music

Do not capitalize the names of seasons, academic disciplines (unless they are languages), or job titles used without a proper noun.

35b ITALICS

Italicize the titles of entire works (books, magazines, newspapers, films), but place the titles of parts of entire works within quotation marks. When italicizing is difficult because you are using a typewriter or writing by hand, underline the titles of entire works instead. Also italicize or underline the names of ships and aircraft.

I am fond of reading *USA Today* in the morning.

The exceptions. Do not italicize or underline the names of sacred texts.

Italicize unfamiliar foreign words

Italicize foreign words that are not part of common English usage. Do not italicize words that have become a common word or phrase in the English vocabulary. How do you decide which words are common? If a word appears in a standard English dictionary, it can be considered as adopted into English.

Use italics to clarify your use of a word, letter, or number

In everyday speech, we often use cues—a pause, a louder or different tone—to communicate how we are using a word. In writing, italics help clarify when you use words in a referential manner, or letters and numbers as letters and numbers.

35c ABBREVIATIONS

Abbreviations are shortened forms of words. Because abbreviations vary widely, you will need to look in the dictionary to determine how to abbreviate words on a case-by-case basis. Nonetheless, there are a few patterns that abbreviations follow.

Abbreviate titles before and degrees after full names

Ms. Ella Fitzgerald
Prof. Vijay Aggarwal

Write out the professional title when it is used with only a last name.

Professor Chin

Reverend Ames

Conventions for using abbreviations with years and times

BCE (before the common era) and CE (common era) are now preferred for indicating years, replacing BC (before Christ) and AD (*anno Domini* ["the year of our Lord"]). Note that all are now used without periods.

479 **BCE** (or BC)

1610 **CE** (or AD, but AD is placed before the number)

The preferred written conventions for times are a.m. (*ante meridiem*) and p.m. (*post meridiem*).

9:03 **a.m.**

3:30 **p.m.**

Conventions for using abbreviations in formal writing

Most abbreviations are inappropriate in formal writing except when the reader would be more familiar with the abbreviation than with the words it represents. When your reader is unlikely to be familiar with an abbreviation, spell out the term, followed by the abbreviation in parentheses, the first time you use it in a paper. The reader will then understand what the abbreviation refers to, and you may use the abbreviation in subsequent sentences.

The **Office of Civil Rights (OCR)** is the agency that enforces Title IX regulations. In 1979, **OCR** set out three options for schools to comply with Title IX.

35d ACRONYMS

Acronyms are abbreviations formed by capitalizing the first letter in each word. Unlike abbreviations, acronyms are pronounced as words.

AIDS for Acquired Immunodeficiency Syndrome

NASA for National Air and Space Administration

A subset of acronyms are initial-letter abbreviations that have become so common that we know the organization or thing by its initials.

ACLU for American Civil Liberties Union

HIV for human immunodeficiency virus

rpm for revolutions per minute

Familiar acronyms and initial-letter abbreviations such as CBS, CIA, FBI, IQ, and UN are rarely spelled out. Unfamiliar acronyms and abbreviations should always be spelled out. Acronyms and abbreviations frequent in particular fields should be spelled out on first use. For example, MMPI (Minnesota Multiphasic Personality Inventory) is a familiar abbreviation in psychology but is unfamiliar to those outside that discipline. Even when acronyms are generally familiar, few readers will object to your giving the terms from which an acronym derives on the first use.

35e NUMBERS

In formal writing spell out any number that can be expressed in one or two words, as well as any number, regardless of length, at the beginning of a sentence. Also, hyphenate two-word numbers from twenty-one to ninety-nine. When a sentence begins with a number that requires more than two words, revise it if possible.

The exceptions. In scientific reports and some business writing that requires the frequent use of numbers, using numerals more often is appropriate. Most styles do not write out in words a year, a date, an address, a page number, the time of day, decimals, sums of money, phone numbers, rates of speed, or the scene and act of a play. Use numerals instead.

In **2001** only **33%** of respondents said they were satisfied with the City Council's proposals to help the homeless.

The **17** trials were conducted at temperatures **12-14°C** with results ranging from **2.43** to **2.89** mg/dl.

When one number modifies another number, write one out and express the other in numeral form.

In the last year all **four 8th** Street restaurants have begun to donate their leftovers to the soup kitchen.

Only after Meryl had run in **12 fifty**-mile ultramarathons did she finally win first place in her age group.

GLOSSARY OF GRAMMATICAL TERMS AND USAGE

The glossary gives the definitions of grammatical terms and items of usage. The grammatical terms are shown in **blue**. Some of the explanations of usage that follow are not rules, but guidelines to keep in mind for academic and professional writing. In these formal contexts, the safest course is to avoid words that are described as *nonstandard, informal,* or *colloquial.*

a/an   Use *a* before words that begin with a consonant sound (*a train, a house*). Use *an* before words that begin with a vowel sound (*an airplane, an hour*).

a lot/alot   *A lot* is generally regarded as informal; *alot* is nonstandard.

accept/except   *Accept* is a verb meaning "receive" or "approve." *Except* is sometimes a verb meaning "leave out," but much more often, it's used as a conjunction or preposition meaning "other than."

active   A clause with a transitive verb in which the subject is the doer of the action (see Section 18a). See also **passive.**

adjective   A modifier that qualifies or describes the qualities of a noun or pronoun (see Sections 27a and 27b).

adjective clause   A subordinate clause that modifies a noun or pronoun and is usually introduced by a relative pronoun (see Section 32c). Sometimes called a *relative clause.*

adverb   A word that modifies a verb, another modifier, or a clause (see Sections 27a, and 27c).

adverb clause   A subordinate clause that functions as an adverb by modifying a verb, another modifier, or a clause (see Section 27c).

advice/advise   The noun *advice* means a "suggestion"; the verb *advise* means to "recommend" or "give advice."

affect/effect   Usually, *affect* is a verb (to "influence") and *effect* is a noun (a "result"). Less commonly, *affect* is used as a noun and *effect* as a verb.

agreement   The number and person of a subject and verb must match—singular subjects with singular verbs, plural subjects with plural verbs (see Chapter 23). Likewise, the number and gender of a pronoun and its antecedent must match (see Section 25b).

all ready/already   The adjective phrase *all ready* means "completely prepared"; the adverb *already* means "previously."

all right/alright   *All right,* meaning "acceptable," is the correct spelling. *Alright* is nonstandard.

allude/elude   *Allude* means "refer to indirectly." *Elude* means "evade."

allusion/illusion   An *allusion* is an indirect reference; an *illusion* is a false impression.

among/between   *Between* refers to precisely two people or things; *among* refers to three or more.

amount/number   Use *amount* with things that cannot be counted; use *number* with things that can be counted.

an   See **a/an.**

antecedent   The noun (or pronoun) that a pronoun refers to (see Section 25b).

anybody/any body; anyone/any one   *Anybody* and *anyone* are indefinite pronouns and have the same meaning; *any body* and *any one* are usually followed by a noun that they modify.

anymore/any more   *Anymore* means "now," while *any more* means "no more." Both are used in negative constructions.

anyway/anyways   *Anyway* is correct. *Anyways* is nonstandard.

articles   The words *a, an,* and *the* (see Section 28b).

as/as if/as though/like   Use *as* instead of *like* before dependent clauses (which include a subject and verb). Use *like* before a noun or a pronoun.

assure/ensure/insure   *Assure* means "promise," *ensure* means "make certain," and *insure* means to "make certain in either a legal or financial sense."

auxiliary verb   Forms of *be, do,* and *have* combine with verbs to indicate tense and mood (see Section 28c). The modal verbs *can, could, may, might, must, shall, should, will,* and *would* are a subset of auxiliaries.

bad/badly   Use *bad* only as an adjective. *Badly* is the adverb.

being as/being that   Both constructions are colloquial and awkward substitutes for *because.* Don't use them in formal writing.

beside/besides   *Beside* means "next to." *Besides* means "in addition to" or "except."

between   See **among/between.**

bring/take   *Bring* describes movement from a more distant location to a nearer one. *Take* describes movement away.

can/may   In formal writing, *can* indicates ability or capacity, while *may* indicates permission.

case   The form of a noun or pronoun that indicates its function. Nouns change case only to show possession: the **dog**, the **dog's** bowl. See **pronoun case.** (Section 25a).

censor/censure   To *censor* is to edit or ban on moral or political grounds. To *censure* is to reprimand publicly.

cite/sight/site   To *cite* is to "mention specifically"; *sight* as a verb means to "observe" and as a noun refers to "vision"; *site* is most commonly used as a noun that means "location," but is also used as a verb to mean "situate."

clause   A group of words with a subject and a predicate. A main or independent clause can stand as a sentence. A subordinate or dependent clause must be attached to a main clause to form a sentence (see Section 22a).

collective noun   A noun that refers to a group or a plurality, such as *team, army,* or *committee* (see Section 23d).

comma splice   Two independent clauses joined incorrectly by a comma (see Section 22c).

common noun   A noun that names a general group, person, place, or thing (see Section 28a). Common nouns are not capitalized unless they begin a sentence.

complement   A word or group of words that completes the predicate. See also **linking verb.**

complement/compliment   To *complement* something is to complete it or make it perfect; to *compliment* is to flatter.

complex sentence   A sentence that contains at least one subordinate clause attached to a main clause.

compound sentence   A sentence that contains at least two main clauses.

compound–complex sentence   A sentence that contains at least two main clauses and one subordinate clause.

conjunction   See **coordinating conjunction** and **subordinating conjunction.**

conjunctive adverb   An adverb that often modifies entire clauses and sentences, such as *also, consequently, however, indeed, instead, moreover, nevertheless, otherwise, similarly,* and *therefore* (see Section 27c).

continual/continuous   *Continual* refers to a repeated activity; *continuous* refers to an ongoing, unceasing activity.

coordinate   A relationship of equal importance, in terms of either grammar or meaning (see Section 20c).

coordinating conjunction   A word that links two equivalent grammatical elements, such as *and, but, or, yet, nor, for,* and *so.*

could of   Nonstandard. See **have/of**.

count noun   A noun that names things that can be counted, such as *block, cat,* and *toy* (see Section 28a).

dangling modifier   A modifier that is not clearly attached to what it modifies (see Section 27e).

data   The plural form of *datum;* it takes plural verb forms.

declarative   A sentence that makes a statement.

dependent clause   See **subordinate clause**.

determiners   Words that initiate noun phrases, including possessive nouns (*Pedro's violin*); possessive pronouns (*my, your*); demonstrative pronouns (*this, that*); and indefinite pronouns (*all, both, many*).

differ from/differ with   To *differ from* means to "be unlike"; to *differ with* means to "disagree."

different from/different than   Use *different from* where possible.

Dark French roast is **different from** ordinary coffee.

direct object   A noun, pronoun, or noun clause that names who or what receives the action of a transitive verb.

discreet/discrete   Both are adjectives. *Discreet* means "prudent" or "tactful"; *discrete* means "separate."

disinterested/uninterested   *Disinterested* is often misused to mean *uninterested.* Disinterested means "impartial." A judge can be interested in a case but disinterested in the outcome.

double negative   The incorrect use of two negatives to signal the same negative meaning.

due to the fact that   Avoid this wordy substitute for *because.*

each other/one another   Use *each other* for two; use *one another* for more than two.

effect   See **affect/effect**.

elicit/illicit   The verb *elicit* means to "draw out." The adjective *illicit* means "unlawful."

emigrate from/immigrate to   *Emigrate* means to "leave one's country"; *immigrate* means to "settle in another country."

ensure   See **assure/ensure/insure**.

enthused   Nonstandard in academic and professional writing. Use *enthusiastic* instead.

etc.   Avoid this abbreviation for the Latin *et cetera* in formal writing. Either list all the items or use an English phrase such as *and so forth*.

every body/everybody; every one/everyone   *Everybody* and *everyone* are indefinite pronouns referring to all people under discussion. *Every one* and *every body* are adjective-noun combinations referring to all members of a group.

except   See **accept/except**.

except for the fact that   Avoid this wordy substitute for *except that*.

expletive   The dummy subjects *it* and *there* used to fill a grammatical slot in a sentence. *It is raining outside. There should be a law against it.*

explicit/implicit   Both are adjectives; *explicit* means "stated outright," while *implicit* means just the opposite, "unstated."

farther/further   *Farther* refers to physical distance; *further* refers to time or other abstract concepts.

fewer/less   Use *fewer* with what can be counted and *less* with what cannot be counted.

flunk   In formal writing, avoid this colloquial substitute for *fail*.

fragment   A group of words beginning with a capital letter and ending with a period that looks like a sentence but lacks a subject or a predicate or both (see Section 22a).

further   See **farther/further**.

gerund   An *-ing* form of a verb used as a noun, such as *running, skiing,* or *laughing*.

good/well   *Good* is an adjective and is not interchangeable with the adverb *well*. The one exception is health. Both she feels *good* and she feels *well* are correct.

hanged/hung   Use *hanged* to refer only to executions; *hung* is used for all other instances.

have/of   *Have,* not *of,* follows *should, could, would, may, must,* and *might.*

he/she; s/he   Try to avoid language that appears to exclude either gender (unless this is intended, of course) and awkward compromises such as *he/she* or *s/he*. The best solution is to make pronouns plural (the gender-neutral *they*) wherever possible (see Section 25c).

helping verb   See **auxiliary verb**.

hopefully   This adverb is commonly used as a sentence modifier, but many readers object to it.

illusion   See **allusion/illusion**.

immigrate   See **emigrate from/immigrate to**.

imperative   A sentence that expresses a command. Usually the subject is implied rather than stated.

implicit   See **explicit/implicit**.

imply/infer   *Imply* means to "suggest"; *infer* means to "draw a conclusion."

in regards to   Avoid this wordy substitute for *regarding*.

incredible/incredulous   *Incredible* means "unbelievable"; *incredulous* means "not believing."

independent clause   See **main clause**.

indirect object   A noun, pronoun, or noun clause that names who or what is affected by the action of a transitive verb.

infinitive   The word *to* plus the base verb form: *to believe, to feel, to act*. See also **split infinitive**.

infinitive phrase   A phrase that uses the infinitive form of a verb.

interjection   A word expressing feeling that is grammatically unconnected to a sentence, such as *cool, wow, ouch,* or *yikes*.

interrogative   A sentence that asks a question.

intransitive verb   A verb that does not take an object, such as *sleep, appear,* or *laugh* (see Sections 24c and 28c).

irregardless   Nonstandard for *regardless*.

irregular verb   A verb that does not use either *-d* or *-ed* to form the past tense and past participle (see Section 24b).

it is my opinion that Avoid this wordy substitute for *I believe that*.

its/it's *Its* is the possessive of *it* and does not take an apostrophe; *it's* is the contraction for *it is*.

-ize/-wise The suffix *-ize* changes a noun or adjective into a verb (*harmony, harmonize*). The suffix *-wise* changes a noun or adjective into an adverb (*clock, clockwise*). Some writers are tempted to use these suffixes to convert almost any word into an adverb or verb form. Unless the word appears in a dictionary, don't use it.

kind of/sort of/type of Avoid using these colloquial expressions if you mean *somewhat* or *rather*. *It's kind of hot* is nonstandard. Each is permissible, however, when it refers to a classification of an object. Be sure that it agrees in number with the object it is modifying.

lay/lie *Lay* means "place" or "put" and generally takes a direct object (see Section 24c). Its main forms are *lay, laid, laid*. *Lie* means "recline" or "be positioned" and does not take an object. Its main forms are *lie, lay, lain*.

less See **fewer**.

lie See **lay/lie**.

linking verb A verb that connects the subject to the complement, such as *appear, be, feel, look, seem,* or *taste*.

lots/lots of Nonstandard in formal writing; use *many* or *much* instead.

main clause A group of words with a subject and a predicate that can stand alone as a sentence. Also called an *independent clause*.

mankind This term offends some readers and is outdated. Use *humans, humanity,* or *people* instead.

may/can See **can/may**.

may be/maybe *May be* is a verb phrase; *maybe* is an adverb.

media This is the plural form of the noun *medium* and requires a plural verb.

might of See **have/of**.

modal A kind of auxiliary verb that indicates ability, permission, intention, obligation, or probability, such as *can, could, may, might, must, shall, should, will,* or *would*.

modifier A general term for adjectives, adverbs, phrases, and clauses that describe other words (see Chapter 27).

must of See **have/of**.

noncount noun   A noun that names things that cannot be counted, such as *air, energy,* or *water* (see Section 28a).

nonrestrictive modifier   A modifier that is not essential to the meaning of the word, phrase, or clause it modifies and should be set off by commas or other punctuation (see Section 29c).

noun   The name of a person, place, thing, concept, or action. See also **common noun** and **proper noun** (see Section 28a).

noun clause   A subordinate clause that functions as a noun.

number   See **amount/number**.

object   Receiver of the action within the clause or phrase.

OK, O.K., okay   Informal; avoid using in academic and professional writing. Each spelling is accepted in informal usage.

owing to the fact that   Avoid this wordy, colloquial substitute for *because*.

parallelism   The principle of putting similar elements or ideas in similar grammatical form (see Section 20c).

participle   A form of a verb that uses *-ing* in the present (*laughing, playing*) and usually *-ed* or *-en* in the past (*laughed, played*). See Section 24a. Participles are either part of the verb phrase (*She had played the game before*) or used as adjectives (*the laughing girl*).

participial phrase   A phrase formed either by a present participle (for example, *racing*) or by a past participle (for example, *taken*).

parts of speech   The eight classes of words according to their grammatical function: nouns, pronouns, verbs, adjectives, adverbs, prepositions, conjunctions, and interjections.

passive   A clause with a transitive verb in which the subject is being acted upon (see Section 18a). See also **active**.

people/persons   *People* refers to a general group; *persons* refers to a collection of individuals. Use *people* over *persons* except when you're emphasizing the idea of separate persons within the group.

per   Try to use the English equivalent of this Latin word except in technical writing or familiar usages like *miles per gallon*.

phenomena   This is the plural form of *phenomenon* ("observable fact" or "unusual event") and takes plural verbs.

phrase   A group of words that does not contain both a subject and predicate.

plenty   In academic and professional writing, avoid this colloquial substitute for *very.*

plus   Do not use *plus* to join clauses or sentences. Use *and, also, moreover, furthermore,* or another conjunctive adverb instead.

precede/proceed   Both are verbs but they have different meanings: *precede* means "come before," and *proceed* means "go ahead" or "continue."

predicate   The part of the clause that expresses the action or tells something about the subject. The predicate includes the verb and all its complements, objects, and modifiers.

prejudice/prejudiced   *Prejudice* is a noun; *prejudiced* is an adjective.

preposition   A class of words that indicate relationships and qualities.

prepositional phrase   A phrase formed by a preposition and its object, including the modifiers of its object.

pronoun   A word that stands for other nouns or pronouns. Pronouns have several subclasses, including personal pronouns, possessive pronouns, demonstrative pronouns, indefinite pronouns, relative pronouns, interrogative pronouns, reflexive pronouns, and reciprocal pronouns (Chapter 25).

pronoun case   Pronouns that function as the subjects of sentences are in the **subjective** case (*I, you, he, she, it, we, they*). Pronouns that function as direct or indirect objects are in the **objective** case (*me, you, him, her, it, us, them*). Pronouns that indicate ownership are in the **possessive** case (*my, your, his, her, its, our, their*) (see Section 25a).

proper noun   A noun that names a particular person, place, thing, or group (see Section 28a). Proper nouns are capitalized.

question as to whether/question of whether   Avoid these wordy substitutes for *whether.*

raise/rise   The verb *raise* means "lift up" and takes a direct object. Its main forms are *raise, raised, raised.* The verb *rise* means "get up" and does not take a direct object. Its main forms are *rise, rose, risen.*

real/really   Avoid using *real* as if it were an adverb. *Really* is an adverb; *real* is an adjective.

reason is because   Omit either *reason is* or *because* when explaining causality.

reason why   Avoid using this redundant combination.

relative pronoun   A pronoun that initiates clauses, such as *that, which, what, who, whom,* or *whose.*

restrictive modifier   A modifier that is essential to the meaning of the word, phrase, or clause it modifies (see Section 29c). Restrictive modifiers are usually not set off by punctuation.

rise/raise   See **raise/rise**.

run–on sentence   Two main clauses fused together without punctuation or a conjunction, appearing as one sentence (see Section 22b).

sentence   A grammatically independent group of words that contains at least one main clause.

sentence fragment   See **fragment**.

set/sit   *Set* means "put" and takes a direct object; its main forms are *set, set, set. Sit* means "be seated" and does not take a direct object; its main forms are *sit, sat, sat. Sit* should not be used as a synonym for *set*.

shall/will   *Shall* is used most often in first person questions, while *will* is a future tense helping verb for all persons. British English consistently uses *shall* with first person: *I shall, we shall*.

should of   See **have/of**.

sit/set   See **set/sit**.

some time/sometime/sometimes   *Some time* means "a span of time," *sometime* means "at some unspecified time," and *sometimes* means "occasionally."

somebody/some body; someone/some one   *Somebody* and *someone* are indefinite pronouns and have the same meaning. In *some body, body* is a noun modified by *some,* and in *some one, one* is a pronoun or adjective modified by *some*.

sort of   See **kind of/sort of/type of**.

split infinitive   An infinitive with a word or words between *to* and the base verb form, such as *to boldly go, to better appreciate* (see Section 27d).

stationary/stationery   *Stationary* means "motionless"; *stationery* means "writing paper."

subject   A noun, pronoun, or noun phrase that identifies what the clause is about and connects with the predicate.

subject–verb agreement   See **agreement**.

subordinate   A relationship of unequal importance, in terms of either grammar or meaning (see Section 20a).

subordinate clause   A clause that cannot stand alone but must be attached to a main clause. Also called a *dependent clause*.

subordinating conjunction   A word that introduces a subordinate clause. Common subordinating conjunctions are *after, although, as, because, before, if, since, that, unless, until, when, where,* and *while.*

such   Avoid using *such* as a synonym for *very.* It should always be followed by a *that* and a clause that contains a result.

sure   A colloquial term used as an adverb to mean "certainly." Avoid using it this way in formal writing.

sure and/sure to; try and/try to   *Sure to* and *try to* are correct; do not use *and* after *sure* or *try.*

take   See **bring/take**.

that/which   *That* introduces a restrictive or essential clause. Restrictive clauses describe an object that must be that particular object and no other. Though some writers occasionally use *which* with restrictive clauses, it is most often used to introduce nonrestrictive clauses. These are clauses that contain additional nonessential information about the object.

transition   A word or phrase that notes movement from one unit of writing to another.

transitive verb   A verb that takes a direct object (see Section 24c).

verb   A word that expresses action or characterizes the subject in some way. Verbs can show tense and mood (see Chapter 24 and Section 28c).

verbal   A form of a verb used as an adjective, adverb, or noun. See also **gerund, infinitive, participle**.

well/good   See **good/well**.

which/that   See **that/which**.

who/whom   *Who* and *whom* follow the same rules as other pronouns: *Who* is the subject pronoun; *whom* is the object pronoun (see Section 36a).

will/shall   See **shall/will**.

-wise/-ize   See **-ize/-wise**.

would of   See **have/of**.

you   Avoid indefinite uses of *you*. It should only be used to mean "you, the reader."

your/you're   The two are not interchangeable. *Your* is the possessive form of "you"; *you're* is the contraction of "you are."

CREDITS

Revision Guide

Commonly used editing and proofreading symbols are listed here, along with references to the relevant chapters and sections of this handbook.

Words, Sentences, and Paragraphs

abbr	Abbreviation problem: 35c	*p*	Punctuation problem: 29-34
adj	Adjective problem: 27a-b	*pass*	Passive voice misused: 18a
adv	Adverb problem: 27a, 27c	*pl*	Plural form misused or needed: 28a
agr	Agreement problem, either subject-verb or pronoun-antecedent: 23, 25b	*pron*	Pronoun problem: 25
		ref	Reference of a pronoun unclear: 25d
apos	Apostrophe missing or misused: 32	*run-on*	Run-on sentence problem: 22b
art	Article is missing or misused: 28b	*sexist*	Sexist language: 21e
cap	Capitalization is needed: 35a	*sp*	Spelling needs to be checked: 7d
case	Case of a pronoun is incorrect: 25a	*sub*	Subordination is faulty: 20a
coh	Coherence lacking in a paragraph: 6a	*trans*	Transition misused or needed: 6b
		vb	Verb problem: 24
cs	Comma splice occurs: 22c	*w*	Wordy: 19
dm	Dangling modifier appears: 27e	*ww*	Wrong word: 21
frag	Fragment instead of complete sentence: 22a	¶	Paragraph break needed: 6
		no ¶	No paragraph break needed: 6b
ital	Italics missing or misused: 35b		
lc	Lower case needed: 35a	//	Parallelism needs to be checked: 20c
mm	Misplaced modifier: 27b-c		
num	Number problem: 35e		

Punctuation and Mechanics

⋏	Comma needed: 29	( )	Parentheses needed: 31
⌄′	Apostrophe needed: 32	[ ]	Brackets needed: 34d
⌄ ⌄	Quotation marks needed: 33	#	Add a space
⊙	Period needed: 34a	⌒	Close up a space
?	Question mark needed: 34b	⟿	Delete this
!	Exclamation point needed: 34c	⋀	Insert something
–	Dash needed: 31	⌢	Transpose (switch the order)
. . .	Ellipses needed: 34e		

Contents

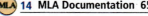